NARROW BOAT PAINTING

NARROW BOAT PAINTING

*A history and description of
the English narrow boats' traditional paintwork*

With 8pp of Colour Plates

A. J. LEWERY

DAVID & CHARLES
NEWTON ABBOT   LONDON

British Library Cataloguing in Publication Data

Lewery, A. J.
  Narrow boat painting.
  1. Canal-boats   2. Decoration and ornament,
  English   3. Inland waterway vessels—England
  I. Title
  623.8′245   TC765

ISBN: 978-1-4463-0653-6

First published 1974
Second impression 1979
Third impression 1983
Fourth impression 1991

Printed in Great Britain
by Redwood Press Ltd, Melksham, Wiltshire
for David & Charles
Brunel House   Newton Abbot   Devon

Contents

List of Illustrations

7

Photographs not acknowledged are from the author's collection.

9

Fig. 1 *A pair of Pickford's narrow boats with a barge on the Thames, part of an etching drawn in 1828 by E. W. Cooke whose work is regarded by marine historians as precise evidence. It gives us some detail of the decoration of the top plank of the hull and the use of diamonds on the door panels, perhaps as part of Pickford's livery.*

CHAPTER I

The Boats and the Boatmen

The narrow boat is the most characteristic craft of the English canals. There were many other types of canal barge, but they were built for localised parts of the waterway system, to measurements which prevent them from leaving their own area. All long-distance canal traffic must therefore be carried in narrow boats, 70 ft long but only 6 ft 10 in to 7 ft wide and built to pass through the narrow locks of the connecting Midland canals.

Before the opening of these narrow gauge canals, the majority of British inland navigations were natural rivers, some deepened or improved by artificial cuts, or short canals that acted as extensions to a river navigation. Naturally these canals were built to accommodate existing local river traffic and there were no standard dimensions. The forefathers of the strictly inland narrow boat are thus found in the barges and boats working on the rivers in the middle of the eighteenth century, and one extreme possibility is that some of the decorative traditions stem from the same root.

The River Mersey seems the most likely development area, as a very early canal, the Sankey Brook Navigation, was linked to it, was designed for use by the existing Mersey sailing flats. The Duke of Bridgewater's canal too, although using tiny boats in and out of the Worsley mine tunnels, was built to a broad gauge to take Mersey flats anticipating a later link with the Mersey at Runcorn. James Brindley's proposals for the Trent & Mersey canal, already being pressed by 1766 suggested the use of narrow boats, built to the measurements that we know today, so perhaps they developed as a cross between the little mine boats and the Mersey sailing flats.

The first spate of canal building, set off by the success of the

Bridgewater canal, partly opened in 1761, had eased by 1772 and there was a lull in developments while work already in progress was completed, and results assessed. After the opening of a country-wide network, the future success of canal transport was assured, and the years 1792–4 saw the start of an incredible number of canal projects, a period known as the time of 'canal mania'.

The great expansion period ended with the construction of the Grand Junction Canal, much later to become the main line of the Grand Union, which was opened in 1805; no more main routes were started after this date with the exception of the Birmingham

Fig. 2 *Detail drawn from a painting of about 1820 in the Museum of British Transport, Clapham. The* Hope *is painted in a red and blue colour scheme, separated by yellow borders, and has the cabin side and the top of the rudder painted white. Diamond patterns seem to be missing but the bright colours are already present.*

& Liverpool Junction, soon to become the largest part of the Shropshire Union system. This was promoted in 1826, by which time the need for direct, fast communication was apparent, particularly with possible railway competition emerging. It was much straighter than the earlier contour canals and made more use of cuttings and embankments to save distance, keeping the locks concentrated in flights, and to a minimum.

Alas, the effort was too little and too late. The success of the Stockton & Darlington Railway in 1825 encouraged others to promote lines in direct competition with existing water routes, and the next 25 years saw a slow but bitter struggle with canal interests opposing railway promoters at every turn. When it finished, a quarter of the waterway system was under direct control of railway interests; some canals had converted themselves into railways or had decided to build their own. The remainder fought back but lost ground in a price-cutting war. The capital necessary for straightening and improving their routes to put them on a competitive footing was not available and some railway-owned canals, sometimes a prominent link in a long distance chain, followed a positively obstructive policy for a few important years. With the proprietors losing heart, a decline set in.

The canal craft carrying much of this coveted traffic had by this time settled firmly into the style that we recognise today as characteristic of the narrow boat. The extremely narrow beam was presumably suggested by Brindley to restrict the size and cost of the proposed Harecastle tunnel. It also meant that the boats could pass in a narrower channel, again saving on construction costs. They had to be strong enough for their hard work, combining the maximum carrying capacity with an ability to travel at a reasonable speed with the minimum of motive power. The result that developed from these requirements was the horse-drawn narrow boat, worked as an economic unit for nearly 200 years. The essential requirement that the boat should travel or 'swim' easily and steer well accounts for the development of the beautiful and graceful fore and stern ends of an otherwise square sectioned box. These craft are absolutely utilitarian, but like most objects

1 *Horse drawn boats at the Anderton lift during the 1930s, waiting to go down and load pottery materials on the River Weaver. The black and white cabin sides were soon to alter to red, yellow and green.*

that are honestly designed, developed and built to do their job with the greatest efficiency, they are beautiful.

In more recent years, the original type was altered and brought up to date. Iron and steel largely replaced wood for the hull, and the introduction of steam engines and later (and more widespread) the internal combustion engine, necessitated the development of the motor boat as a distinct craft. A motor boat has a lower carrying capacity, 21 or 22 tons being a good load, but enough power was provided to propel itself along and to tow another boat behind it. This means that the two people required to work a horse boat, one to drive the horse and one to steer, could now work and transport twice the load at the same speed as with one horse boat before, a system widely adopted as the most economic method of working narrow boats. A great advantage of having the motor boat towing a 'butty', as the dumb-boat is called, is that they may be singled out and worked independently through the narrow (7 ft) locks, or tied abreast of each other and worked through the wide (or barge) locks as one boat with the consequent saving of both labour and water.

An important date with reference to the history of the narrow boat must be 1789. In that year the Oxford Canal was opened to traffic, completing a cross-country network that allowed long distance traffic from Manchester to travel via the Midlands, to London without trans-shipment. This through network had been envisaged by Brindley as early as 1766 when the Acts of Parliament for the building of the Trent & Mersey Canal, opened in 1777, and the Staffordshire & Worcestershire Canal, opened in 1772, were granted. From those dates we can assume that the narrow boat with a living cabin for a full time crew became common.

The relatively good wages offered during the canals' prosperous first phase ensured an adequate all-male work force. A captain was employed for each boat who then had to find and pay for the necessary mate, another man or boy. It is not clear when women started to work on the boats regularly but they were certainly there in small numbers by 1800. It seems that whenever circumstances forced a cutback in trade or wages, the incidence of women working the canals rose, presumably as the boatmen then took their wives or girlfriends along to save the expense of a paid crew. This was not necessarily regarded as a permanent arrangement, but just as a stop-gap to get the boat owner or captain over a bad patch. We can suppose, though, that some of the women found the life to their liking and did not return to the bank after the trade crisis had passed.

One such crisis was the price-cutting war that was part of the strong railway competition, and the practice of taking the wife along as crew became more common. Many families moved, lock, stock and barrel, on to the boats, but the majority still managed to keep their houses ashore, although they might be unused for 90 per cent of the time. Between the two world wars and during the rundown of narrow boats since the last war, the wages of boatmen would not stretch to maintaining two homes, and the relatively

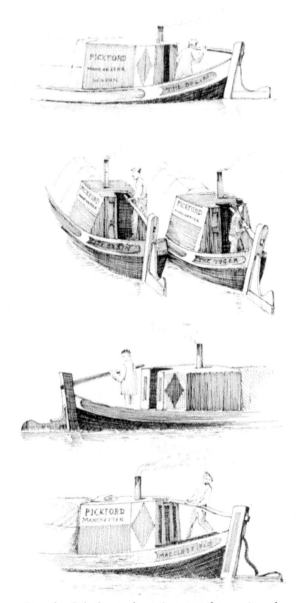

Fig. 3 *Details of the boats shown in a set of engravings drawn by Thomas Shepherd in 1827. The standard treatment of the top planks is again clearly stated and the use of the big diamond on the cabin side suggesting a Pickford's trademark. If it was it would be a good starting point for the later narrow boat diamond patterns as it would have lost any special allegiance when Pickford's ceased carrying by canal in the 1840s.*

few people working the boats during the last 40 years have used their boats as their permanent and only homes.

With the coming of the women to the canal, we would expect to see the beginning of a different, feminine standard of cleanliness and extra decoration on the boats. The houseproud wives off the land were hardly likely to put up with, for very long, the spartan conditions under which their men had worked. A working boatman, however proud of his boat, would not have gone to much trouble to create a home for himself while he had a pleasant house ashore, but when this was gone and his wife joined him, it had to be made as pleasant as possible to be bearable and a refuge from its surroundings. This sounds a little odd when one considers the canals cutting and winding through pleasant countryside, but it was the construction of the canals and the cheaper transport of raw materials that caused the rapid expansion of large centres of industry, and it is here that the boats would be tied for any free or waiting time; the numerous wharves of Birmingham, Paddington, Manchester and the Potteries would be the most usual scene outside. Even in the country, the newly cut canals can hardly have been called beautiful until nature softened them. Is it altogether surprising that the cabins became a positive riot of decoration in defence, and that the people should try to disguise the utilitarian nature of their homes with applied arts at their most insistent?

The everyday needs of this floating population were soon catered for along the canalside and the canal society became tighter-knit for, although widespread in linear distance, the boundaries did not need to extend beyond a few yards from the towpath. Being such an insular unit, the group was ripe for the emergence of trade practices and a special boatpeople's code of behaviour. Any group of people who choose, or are forced, to take a style of life so circumscribed, have only a few possessions which, because they are so few, are very important. These articles are not just important in their practical uses, but important in being possessions and thus giving the owner status and preserving the respect of others. It is a natural desire to want to improve the quality of these articles by any means possible, by carving, painting or embroidering them.

19

2 & 3 *These photographs of Preston Brook are fairly typical of the everyday surroundings of the boat people while tied up, loading or unloading. Although scenes of great interest to later historians, there are perhaps better places to live and bring up children, and the delicate overdecoration of the boats may be part of a reaction against their surroundings.*

4 *John and Mrs Beech on their own boat* Willie & Albert *in 1921, tied abreast of a Northwich Carrying Co. boat worked by Mr & Mrs William Johnson. The owner boatman's craft has very intricate decoration, diamonds and stripes on the tiller, fancy lettering on the cabin side and a mass of patterns on the rudder.*

By increasing their superficial value or quality, the lack of actual quantity of goods is less noticeable. This I believe to be the basic reason for the profusion of decoration on both gypsy living wagons and narrow boats. Both groups are limited to a few possessions by their way of life, and both are limited to living in spaces about 10 ft by 6 ft by the practical considerations of road and canal width. Without the added decoration, living happily in such conditions permanently would be more difficult.

Contemporary records of the early days of canal boating are rare. Illustrations that survive seem to be full of artistic licence and need to be translated to make the boats depicted seaworthy, and conform to the actual measurements that we know them to have been.

This lack of information generally makes the earliest reference to canal painting and decoration seem all the more interesting in that it is quite believable and seems extremely closely observed. In a series of three articles in *Household Words* of 1858, the author describes a journey up the Grand Junction Canal on a narrow boat, and notes the way that family boating was becoming very common at that time.* More central to our subject is the description he gives of the painted decoration on the boat, both the use of extremely bright colours for the main areas of paintwork, and the painting of 'landscapes, in which there is a lake, a castle, a sailing boat, and a range of mountains', as well as 'gaudy wreaths of flowers' on the boat and its water can. He mentions these decorations in a way that suggests that they are not at all uncommon on the boats, leading to the conclusion that the whole tradition of boat painting was already set up and operative only 60 years after the beginning of through traffic.

Fig. 4 *This engraving illustrated an article in the* Art Journal *of 1873, and is the earliest showing the use of the castle landscape as a decorative device on narrow boats. It is also satisfyingly clear about the decoration of the top plank and tiller, and the layout of the cabin sides.*

* Appendix 1

The boat population otherwise comes down to us as a hard-working but rough and ready group. Being a fairly large community and constantly on the move, the country let them go their own way about things until a social reformer, George Smith of Coalville, turned his attention towards them. He had previously fought for and won an Act of Parliament bettering the lot of the child labour of the Midlands brickfields, and it was now the plight of the children of the boat people that drew his fanatical sympathy, and started his campaign on their behalf.

Reading his campaigning literature, it is sometimes difficult to believe that the same group of people are also the subject of the article *Life on the Upper Thames*.* No mention by Mr Smith of polished brass, suntan or bright paint and pictures – only a sordid picture of human desolation and misery, with constant drunkenness, illiteracy and vermin, as the day to day existence of the boat population. It is perhaps a timely reminder that the truth could lie somewhere between the two.

The survival of the painting tradition can be attributed partly to the original conception, design and building of the canals. They were so economical as a means of transport that these self-same canals, built between 1780 and 1840 in the main, were still carrying loads alongside modern rail and road transport until 1970. There had been little modernisation on the narrow canals during this time, the boats being almost the same size, carrying the same tonnage, as the boats of 1800. It follows that since the trade survived unchanged, so did the tradesman.

Without modernisation being possible, the boatman lived on his boat and travelled with his family as he had always done since the beginning of family boating. The essential ingredients of a complete society were still there and still on the move. Recently the boatman's working hours were just as long and hard as his grandfather's had been, while nearly all other workers in modern industry were down to a 40-hour week, another fact to be considered when studying the paint, polish and time-consuming traditions of the boats. It is not done to while away the afternoon –

* Appendix 2

time had to be found or made during a busy day's work to keep the brasswork polished, the decorative ropework scrubbed and to keep up the high standards of cleanliness apparent on many craft.

Whatever the origins of canal boat painting, another reason for its survival and development is the boatman's need to restate the separateness of his trade community. As their obvious independence as a group increased the antagonism of the rest of society, so it became necessary to strengthen the trade mystique. A man who feels himself to be part of an exclusive club, rather than a lonely individual, is better able to withstand the gibes of the outsiders, whom he can then claim are merely jealous. The canal boatman still maintains the mystique, albeit unintentional, when he insists that nobody can work a boat really well unless he is born to it, quite regardless of experience. It is pleasantly surprising to find that the tradition of decorative painting was still honestly-based and healthy on the narrow boats until the 1960s. I hope that the following chapters will note and record this fascinating folk tradition before it fades out, or is radically altered by commercialism, as the canals' lifeblood ceases to be transport and becomes pleasure boating.

5 Water Lily *and* Forget me Not, *owned and worked by Edward Powell, are typical of the pairs of horse boats that carried coal on the Grand Junction Canal.*

CHAPTER 2

'Roses and Castles'- Origins

We have arrived then at a relatively small, tightly-knit trade community whose whole history is only 200 years. Yet it developed a complete tradition of painted decoration apparently quite alien to any other group in England, the origins of which seem extremely obscure for such a recent folk art.

The whole subject divides itself into two very different approaches at the first studied glance. The large, bold designs of diamond patterns, hearts, clubs and crescents, which, with the use of strong contrasting colours on separate parts of the boat, make the first, most striking impression, will be discussed later. Overshadowed by this general effect is an entirely different treatment, the painting of romantic pictures and wreaths of flowers on the boats. It is so unlike any other boat decoration and seems so un-English that it has received rather more attention and been given the generic term 'Roses & Castles'.

With the earliest written records that I have been able to discover (Appendices 1, 2, 3) we find with certainty that it was widespread and well established 100 years ago and appears to have been accepted practice in 1858.

This defuses the otherwise believable boatman stories about 'old Fred the lock-keeper, who grew a lot of roses about the place and could see Chirk castle from the garden – he started it all when I was a young man', or that it was invented by a dockyard painter who only died a few years ago. It is interesting, nevertheless, that many boatmen regard it as being so recent, and returns the subject to its rightful place as applied decoration, from the one of religious significance that outsiders sometimes allow it to occupy.

The article from the *Birmingham Daily Mail*, 1875* is also

* See Appendix 3

6 *This 10 ft wide beam craft built to work on the Grand Junction Canal nevertheless highlights the contrasting narrow boat treatments, the delicate roses and castles with the bolder geometric designs.*

interesting in its mention of the painters' subjects – 'a gay cavalier or valiant crusader in full armour'. Although written in a rather generalised and patronising manner, the mention of these two subjects so specifically suggests accurate personal observation. When describing the pail, he mentions 'outrageous roses and sunflowers'. In 1873 Mr Robertson describes the pictures as 'landscapes (usually river scenes)', and John Hollingshead in *Household Words* talks of 'fanciful composition landscapes, (and) several gaudy wreaths of flowers'. All these references give broader boundaries to the subject than the modern term 'roses and castles' allows, and we must use it flexibly when looking for, or suggesting, origins.

The most generally accepted theory sees some connection between Romany gypsies and the boatmen. It is believed that some worked as labourers on the Bridgewater canal, and when it was finished, realised that the job of boatmen on the canal would be quite amenable to their way of life. They would be able to travel with their families, and would be working with horses. The small living space provided by the boat cabin would present no problem to a people used to living in gypsy tents and waggons. The floral decorations would be a continuation of their own style of painting, or an acquired art from the continent where several possibly related styles of decoration are to be found. The castles and landscapes were memory pictures of scenes they had seen in their travels, particularly in the Carpathian mountains, where castles strikingly similar to some of the painted boat castles are found.

If we argue each of these points individually, however, this comfortable theory looks a little thinner. When first opened, the Bridgewater canal was only seven miles long, so that the wanderlust of the gypsy would hardly be satisfied by a four-hour journey. It is also unlikely that the cabin had been considered, as there would be no necessity to sleep aboard on such a short trip. The layout of the narrow boat cabin furnishings does suggest some gypsy connections, as it has some similarities to the Romany waggon; this, though, is a 'chicken or the egg' question, as living waggons were not developed until the mid-nineteenth century. Before this, gypsies were exclusively tent dwellers. Even if they had, much later, appeared on the canals, when there was more extensive navigation throughout the country, a regular seven or eight day run back and forth can hardly be called roaming at will; and horses were then as much everybody's business as the motor car is today.

Another distinction pointing to the absence of gypsy influence is that their favoured decoration is notable for its lack of realistic pictorial content, in contrast to the naturalistic work on the narrow boat. Romany paintwork is nearly always baroque in character, with much rolling, complicated scroll-work; the carved work is in the form of scrolls and stylised acanthus leaves, with birds and animals introduced in a very abstract and symbolic manner. The only realistic painting is of horses, or horses' heads, which are part of the gypsy culture. The whole effect could be an echo of an old mythology, an effect that is entirely missing in boat decoration.

Fig. 5 *Two styles of gypsy waggon decoration, the left-hand one on a Reading waggon built by Dunton's, and the other on a Bill Wright waggon from Leeds. The motifs are late Victorian baroque and contrast strongly with the naive pictures and designs of the narrow boats which predate them.*

A more interesting possibility is that it started with one man, or one family, who felt a need for some rich decoration in the tiny living space and discovered a simple but effective method of representing flowers. The dog-rose would have been an ideal starting point, a flower that was simple, colourful and could be seen regularly all along the hedges. The sophistication of this folk flower to the present style would come about with its spread of popularity amongst the boats. At dockyards throughout the country, there would be full-time painters, who might have had the time and the skill to experiment with the original form and to produce the boat rose that we recognise. If this surmise is correct, it must have happened very early for the style to have become so widespread and generally accepted by the late nineteenth century, when our information becomes more extensive.

In both these discussed viewpoints, the problem of the castles has been sidestepped. Why castles? Although they are not the only subject matter of boat painters, they are by far the most usual and there seems no folk precedent for them, and no obvious symbolic significance. If the gypsies painted them from memory, why the importance of castles? There must have been other impressive sights and scenes during their travels of equal importance in their minds. England is not lacking in castles and stately homes, and if one slides around the original question and merely asks 'which castles?', more local answers come to mind. Most canals have their impressive houses, buildings, castles and eighteenth-century follies to be seen at a little distance; in the beginning of the nineteenth century, with their parkland and landscaped gardens, they must have appeared even more mysterious and fairylike. It has been suggested that the pictures are romantic views of some early factories, with the numerous towers representing chimneys. Combine these ideas with the regular use made of Windsor Castle as a symbol of the monarchy and the expanding empire, and there is no shortage of possible inspirations.

It is because the tradition became so widespread so quickly that it seems likely to me to have had a widespread starting point. Tempting though it is to link the various folk painting styles

7 *A lady's writing cabinet of about 1795, a fine example of Floral decoration on Sheraton furniture.*

and find a tenuous chain threading them together, all the more local and obvious possibilities must be eliminated first. If it had been a true ethnic folk art in the early nineteenth century, one would expect it to be more thoroughly noted. As there is almost a total absence of written records about it, either it did not exist or it was not recognised as anything unusual. John Hollingshead's article proves that it did exist in 1858, so we are left with the other possibility.

The first step was to look again at common furniture of the period and the ideas of high fashion decorators. The heyday for Sheraton designs was the 20 years from 1780 to 1800. Furniture with painted decoration had been introduced by the Adam brothers during the 1760s but Sheraton brought it to its height with pieces decorated with wreaths of flowers and roses, and the occasional use of a decorative panel with classical overtones, figures reclining amongst Greek ruins representing art or music or an abstract theme. This period and the following 20 years or so, during which the ideas of high fashion would have circulated down through the whole of society and the country, was the canal era, during which most of the canals of the country were built. The potential traffic was enormous and profits were magnificent, until the railways' arrival introduced competition. Is it possible that some benevolent canal-owner or carrier hired a furniture painter to decorate his boats, to raise himself in the esteem of his boatmen or as an advertisement for the firm? Or did the boatman himself take the style, then so popular, as his starting point and adopt it as his own?

Admittedly, this whole idea appeared rather far-fetched until examples of early Victorian paintwork were examined and more links became apparent. The undocumented middle grade furniture of the period has largely vanished, leaving us with only the very best, which has been well maintained because of its high initial cost or the well-made country pieces built to last for generations, but with little embellishment. Those chairs and tables that did survive have, by the nature of painted additions, suffered wear or have been repainted, leaving little evidence amongst ordinary household goods. However, there is one group of objects that gives a clearer picture of the taste of these times. At the beginning of the nineteenth century, brass grandfather clock dials gave way to cheaper, painted, iron dials which have left us some beautiful examples of decorative painting.

The long case clock of the eighteenth century had a square brass face, with a silvered or brass chapter circle, or hour ring, applied to it. The corners of the dial outside the chapter circle were then decorated with small, screwed-on castings, usually designs of acanthus foliage in the classical tradition, or cherubs' heads. These corners are called the 'spandrels'. Above the square of the dial there is a semicircle, called the 'arch', which in the more complicated mechanisms, has a cutaway portion revealing another revolving dial showing phases of the moon and the date. This moon disc had always been painted with the moon and night sky for the previous 50 years while in use with brass-faced clocks. With the increased use of a completely painted iron dial, the dial painter, as well as writing the hour and minute numbers, decorated the spandrels and developed the decoration of the arch. During

Fig. 6 *Decoration on grandfather clock dials of the 1820s. The semi-circular picture is the arch design of one clock, whilst the corners show the spandrel design of another.*

the 1820s the favourite spandrel design was a group of flowers, very sophisticated and beautifully done; the painting on the plain arch was, four times out of five, a ruined castle in a landscape containing a river. The spaces between the two moons painted on the separate moon dial usually showed a romantic view including a picturesque ruin on one side and a beautifully executed sailing ship opposite. After the 1840s, this set pattern varied rather more, and the delicacy of the earlier painted dials turns into crude, bad taste at times. Spandrels were painted with anything from rustic sheep and shepherds, through the evergreen castles, to languishing Victorian ladies representing the four seasons, and the only thing that would seem to link them with the canal painters is the very speed and professionalism of their approach.

The constantly recurring theme is the ruined castle, itself a link directly to the renaissance. Following the reappraisal of ancient art and values came a long period of unthinking reverence of anything old and classical, culminating in the final decadence of

32

constructing ruins and classical follies in the gardens of the rich and fashionable. From them, the middle class took their standards and the ruined castle became a symbol, first of classical learning, and lower down, of all that was genteel and 'nice'. Did the boat people take this symbol, without the subtleties, and by adopting it and altering the effect from romantic decay to theatrical security, create a new tradition of decoration? If this train of development did take place, with Kauffman, Cipriani, and Zucchi in the furniture field and Zoffany working on clock dials, the canal painters have some pretty distinguished forefathers.

Once noted, the same decorative fashions appear in several other fields. About 1750, for example, a method of painting and stoving thin iron-sheet was perfected in South Wales that achieved a very glossy and attractive surface, a technique evolved by furniture makers and designers who wished to emulate the lacquer

8 *A little-known area of popular art is glass painting. These slick commercial pictures were very popular around the 1850s; it is thought they were made in the Midlands and may have employed the same class of decorator as the japanning industry, especially as hand painted decoration was then giving ground before mass production methods. Both subject and technique of this one suggest a connection with boat painting.*

finish on the oriental furniture that was then so popular. From their success, the method became known as 'japanning' and it was as *Pontypool and Usk Japanned Ware* that the teapots, coffeepots and trays were advertised and sold in London. They were delicately and beautifully painted, usually with a floral motif, less often with a scene presented as a completed painting, with a tracery of gold lines around the border, and finished to a high standard of craftsmanship. Business boomed and the industry increased, but could not keep pace with demand and the larger producers of tinware in Birmingham and the Black Country moved in on the market. In competition, they introduced mass produced trays and objects with a lower artistic standard, but with correspondingly lower prices, affording a fairly clear example of the way ideas and designs were working down, through competition and lower prices, to the working classes.

9 *This papier-maché tray made in the Black Country in about 1850 illustrates the regular use of the castle as a decorative symbol on better quality goods.*

Almost the same process was happening in the papier-mâché trade in the same area. The same expanding market for imitation oriental goods resulted in several firms developing the manufacture of papier-mâché to a very high standard, but there were many competitors with lower standards.* Cheap mass-produced and gaudy goods of both materials flooded on to the market during the formative years of the boating population. With both of these trades selling objects, particularly tea trays, that were handpainted, but using a very slick commercialised technique to save on labour costs, the comment by Hollingshead in the *Household Words* article, 'a lake, a castle, a sailing boat and a range of mountains painted after the *style of the great teaboard school of art*' takes on new significance.

An interesting example of the way in which these commercial designs gave an impetus to completely fresh folk art forms, can be seen in early American decorative art. Sheraton-style chairs and furniture as well as tinware, were exported extensively to the new country, but so fastgrowing was the young America that these objects served only to generally direct the efforts of the new industries, rather than to control them. The result is rather unexpected. Sheraton chairs, transplanted, blossomed forth as the 'Hitchcock' chair, painted, with the floral decoration transformed to a rather simplified stencil pattern of fruit and flowers, making much use of gold or bronze powders with overlaid glaze colours for the designs. The constrained English furniture rapidly fathered a new tradition of simple, unpretentious furniture in the new country. In the field of tinware, the change was even more pronounced in one area. It gave the new American a splendid, fashionable excuse to paint many of the homemade tinware utensils. In the country districts and particularly in Pennsylvania, where there were many German immigrants, the elegant floral designs became simplified down to a style reminiscent of our own canal painting, with the abstract design of the brush strokes themselves becoming more important as a decorative motif than the floral

* See Appendix 4

Fig. 7 *A Pennsylvanian Dutch brushstroke design, where the pattern of the brushstrokes has become more important than the portrayal of a flower.*

subject. It has become known as 'Pennsylvania Dutch (Deutsch) Brush-Stroke Paintwork', and there is even a suggestion that the earliest examples were an especially 'bad' line painted in England specifically for export. Whether or not there is a connection between this American folk art and canal painting in England, it is easy to believe that they developed at the same time, from the same root sources and for the same fundamental reasons.

Another possibility is that the boatman took his traditional designs from the pottery of the period which, of course, reflected the same design tendencies as the furniture, papier-mâché and tinware. This may well be so; it is certain that there were many pottery decorators with the necessary skill to transpose the designs and paint them on the boats; there is some evidence that these tradesmen moved from ceramic work in the potteries to japanned work in Birmingham just as the trade fluctuated.

My own conclusion is that the juxtaposition of so many skilled

10 *A Braunston-painted water can, showing the decorative quality of the brushstrokes themselves, regardless of the floral idea.*

decorators with possibly the busiest canal area in the country makes the Birmingham-Wolverhampton area the most likely starting point of the canal tradition. This feeling was strengthened when I discovered that most of the painted iron clock dials throughout the country were made and painted in Birmingham, and exported complete. The necessarily large number of tradesmen there puts a different emphasis on the part of the *Household Words* article that mentions 'a new two gallon watercan, shipped from a bankside painter's yard'. It is not necessarily a 'canal painter's' yard on the bank, but could be simply a painter's yard that happened to be on the canal bank. Was a clock dial painter or a japan ornamenter originally employed by the boatmen to bring their utilitarian cabins more into line with current fashion? Admittedly, this is hair splitting. The fundamental fact of importance is the narrow boat world's adoption of these designs, regardless of their previous home and their development to the lovely little folk tradition that we still possess.

11 *A coffee pot of about 1790, made in Stoke-on-Trent or Leeds, with a style of flower decoration that could have contributed to the canal boat tradition.*

CHAPTER 3

𝔇iamonds, 𝔇esigns and 𝔇erivations

Having discussed some possible sources of the roses and castles,
the bolder and more obvious colours and designs should be looked
at in similar depth; again, the difficulty is a multiplicity of possible
sources, rather than a scarcity. It is fairly easy to see the origins
of some individual parts of this painting convention, but much
more difficult to find one source from which it could be derived.
In this section I have worked through the various areas of
decoration on the narrow boat, trying to define the general style,
and the boundaries of what was acceptable, and discussing possible
origins of specific designs as they present themselves.

I   THE FORE END

The first part to be considered as the boat approaches are the
forward 'top bends', which are the top planks of the wooden
hull given a 'tumble home', or tip inwards as they bend round
to meet the stempost. Where the lower edge meets the upper
edge of the more normally bent plank below, there is mounted
a strong iron guard strip, which continues back along the boat
for some feet on the loaded waterline. This strong guard takes
most of the bumps on a normally worked boat, so the first few
feet of the top plank are well protected and by virtue of the boat's
sheer, rise clear of the water and present an ideal ground for
applied decoration.

The paintwork of the top bends falls into a fairly rigid formula,
the centre portion usually being a dark colour, very often red,
edged all round with a $1\frac{1}{2}$ in or 2 in light-coloured line. The centre
section thus echoes the tapering shape of the complete plank with
the resulting border thrown into relief in turn by the black gas-

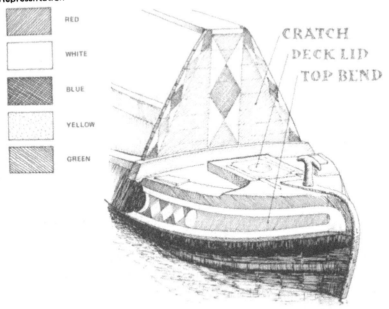

CRATCH

DECK LID

TOP BEND

Fig. 8 *The fore end of a boat in the colours of Cowburn & Cowpar of Manchester.*

tarred hull and guard below, and the dark-coloured paint, usually blue or green, of the capping pieces of the deck above. This simple pattern is the norm from which most other fore-end designs are developed or deviate. Most of the assertions and generalisations in this chapter are made from personal observation and research backed up by photographic evidence, but can therefore only be treated as true for the last 60 or so years; the treatment of the top bends described above nevertheless was widespread in the 1820s, as is evident from the prints of Pickfords' narrow boats. Although of strange proportions, their 'echo' style of decoration is clearly represented.

This technique also illustrates one of the basic unwritten rules of boat painting – light colours against dark wherever possible which, in consequence, makes the paintwork bright and powerful, but never gaudy. The colours used are the monochromatic

Plate I *By alternating light colours with dark the boat painter keeps the* *strong colours in harmony.* (Above): *This horse-drawn tanker, restored to* *its trading colour scheme, preserves some idea of the amount of decoration* *usual on a working narrow boat.* (Below): Jupiter *and* Saturn, *a pair of* *boats converted to passenger carrying, illustrate the characteristic style of* *top bends and deck lid.*

Plate III (Opposite): *A table cupboard door by Bill Hodgson the painter at the Anderton Company Dock in Stoke-on-Trent. His approach to flowers was more artistic than that of most dock painters, and the result more natural.*

Plate II (Below): *A Willow Wren Transport Services butty in 1964, making attractive use of fairly simple, clear cut geometrical designs.*

Plate IV *Two examples of the effect of Hodgson's style on the work of boatman painters. (Left): A water can by Reg Barnett, a boatman with John Whalley, a firm carrying pottery material.*

(Below): A Bridgewater Canal water barrel by Harry Bentley of the Anderton Company. These unwieldy barrels were used where the canal's ample headroom ensured they would not have to be moved very often.

primaries, red, blue and yellow, with green, black and white. Maroon was used as the basic cabinside livery of some firms, but surprisingly, orange paint is very rarely used, and pastel colours hardly ever. Orange is supplanted by the use made of imitation graining as a large colour mass, light oak or cedar wood for first choice. The last colour ingredient to include is red oxide, sometimes called common or raddle-red, with which the cabin roofs, foredecks and the inside of the holds of both steel and wooden boats are generally painted.

The central dark segment of the top bends is then sometimes subdivided by light circles or crescents and the separate parts painted in different colours, though still preserving unbroken the light border; again, part of it may be divided up into a few large diamonds or a mass of smaller ones. A great number of variations have been used, but all conclude with a yellow crescent where the central colour or design meets the black of the hull, with the convex side of the crescent towards the bows.

Like all confident generalisations, there are important exceptions. Boats of the Samuel Barlow Coal Company and the Shropshire Union Company for example had the top bends painted plain white with no echoing centre section. The Barlow boats had a group of flowers on the white ground, and a strange little extended spiky heart shape in red, while the Shropshire Union had one simple black disc on each side, the 'eyes' of a Shropshire Union boat. Had it not been for the Pickford prints one could have expected the standard decoration of top bends to have developed from a plain white area with applied symbols, since the pre-1920 colour scheme of the large canal carriers, Fellows, Morton & Clayton, had a similar simple scheme for the bows.

The name of the boat sometimes appears on the central shape. It was more widespread in the south, where the River Thames regulations required it, and boats of the Willow Wren Carrying Company, the Grand Union fleet and the Ovaltine manufacturers had it as part of their company livery.

It should not surprise us to find the bows decorated in some way, for there is a very strong international tradition among

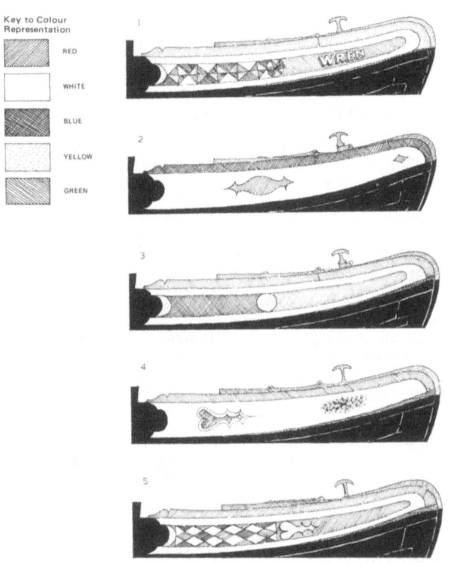

Key to Colour Representation

RED

WHITE

BLUE

YELLOW

GREEN

Fig. 9 *Various decorative treatments of the fore top bends. 1) Willow Wren Canal Transport Services, 2) Fellows, Morton & Clayton Ltd before their colour scheme change in the 1920s, 3) The later FM&C pattern, as well as the basic design on many boats throughout the canal system, 4) Samuel Barlow Coal Company, 5) Henry Grantham, a Grand Junction owner boatman.*

boatmen and boatbuilders to 'give a ship some eyes to see with', called the 'Oculus' tradition. The easy explanation is to assume that the eyes are a symbol of the ship's personal character, but the practice had a different early religious significance. The ancient Egyptians seem to have started it, as a sign that the necessary rites and sacrifices had been made to ensure the ship had the protection of Osiris. This belief in a weakened and altered form became widespread, from the North Atlantic through to the China seas, where it persists strongly as part of Chinese-junk decoration. In Europe it manifests itself best on the prows of Portuguese fishing boats, and in a sanctified way as a five-pointed star on the bows of many continental canal boats.

Fig. 10 *Three Portuguese fishing boats with varying manifestations of the 'Oculus' tradition.*

Disregarding the Oculus tradition, the decoration of the top strake still falls within a historic nautical pattern that extends worldwide. Medieval ships made much use of painted geometrical patterns around the hull from the heraldic use of shields on earlier ships. By the time of Elizabeth I it had developed into a system of abstract paintwork that merely served to finish off the boat and accentuate the lines. A herringbone pattern or a band of diagonal stripes might extend for the whole length of the craft along the top plank or planks of the hull proper, with the raised decks of the fore and stern castles painted in bright geometrical designs. On warships this quickly gave way to more lavish and sophisticated decoration making more use of carving and gold leaf, until it reached heavy and rather unseaworthy heights in the middle of the seventeenth century. How long the system of simple paintwork lasted on the smaller coasters and private ships after 1600 to 1650 is difficult to determine.

The Dutch *bottas*, however, the commonest sailing fishing boats of the Zuider Zee before reclamation made them redundant, make an interesting comparison. The fishermen were fond of using a band pattern of triangles or chevrons to decorate part of the rudders and tillers of their boats. Carried out in the national colours of red, white and blue, it is called *prinswerk* and is a direct descendant of the medieval practice. The contention is that since such patterns continued through to recent fishermen's use in Holland, the diamond patterns of the narrow boat could have a history just as long, with the link provided by some now defunct coastal or fishing craft of the eighteenth or early nineteenth century.

The little foredeck of the narrow boat is usually flat red-oxide paint or red gloss which, although brighter, has the disadvantage of being rather more slippery when wet. The Thos Clayton tar-boats occasionally used flat green paint for the foredeck and the stern cabin roof, but red-oxide was more or less universal. The outer edges of the deck on top of the top planks are protected by capping, or cant pieces, which are usually painted in a dark tone, green or blue, to contrast with the light borders of the top bends already described. In the centre of the foredeck is a hinged hatch cover that allows access to the forepeak, which is stanked off from the rest of the hold and is used as a rope and paint store. This hatch, termed the 'deck lid' is painted white or yellow with a simple symbol in the middle and bordered with a dark colour, the same as the cants. On the boats of the Fellows, Morton & Clayton fleet the deck lid was white, with a red central disc and a straight green edging; this is purely an example, for although Fellows, Morton & Clayton were regarded as setting a standard, the variations were numerous, making use of hearts, diamonds, and ovals, and scalloping the surrounding border. It is, however, usually simpler in design than the sliding hatches used on the stern, living cabin.

II CRATCH, MAST, STANDS AND PLANKS

Access to the foredeck from the stern cabin is made by overlapping gangplanks that run the full length of the boat from cabin to foredeck, supported at intervals along the hold by upright planks, and at the front by a triangular board known as the 'cratch' board. This board and the upright supports, called 'stands', keep the walking planks about 6 or 7 ft above the bottom of the boat and about 2-3 ft above the level of the gunwales, so providing the centre ridgepole for the tentlike shape of the tarpaulins protecting the cargo from the weather.

The cratch board tapers up from the full width of the boat where it sits snugly on the deck beam, to the width of the gangplanks, usually about 3 ft above the foredeck level. All narrow boats engaged in general cargo carrying, including anything that might suffer from the rain, have the cratch covered by a small

12 *Two decorated cratches on* Swan *and* Gertrude *of Gordon Waddington's fleet at Runcorn in 1960, both painted at Lees & Atkins' dock at Polesworth.*

tarpaulin or 'deck-cloth', that is sealed and nailed down to the deck beam, then drawn up and back over the cratch. With the addition of a tarpaulin over the planks, with its forward edge overlapping the deck-cloth, a very weatherproof roof is formed over the hold. Many boats, however, were engaged solely in carrying imperishable goods, like coal and ironstone, where the deck-cloth and subsequent weatherproofing were unnecessary and the cratch board was left exposed; then, instead of red-oxide, or purely preservative paint, the board was often fully decorated.

Latterly all the decorated cratches followed a similar pattern, with a vertical band of diamonds the same width as the gangplanks down the middle, and the remaining triangles on either side bordered and painted with a group of flowers. It seems likely that this formula, although popular, was not without wide variation. A 'Number-One' or owner-boatman development seen in one photograph uses the Union Jack as the motif on each side of the central lozenges.

An oddity that falls within this category of painted cratch boards was the use made of them by the makers of Ovaltine, who owned coal boats. They used the board in a more modern advertising sense, and had their punch line 'Drink Delicious Ovaltine for Health' painted on it in accordance with their normal poster advertising style, in yellow letters on a maroon/brown background.

13 *Cratches used for advertisement rather than decoration on Ovaltine's own pair of boats* William *and* Enid *at their factory in 1956.*

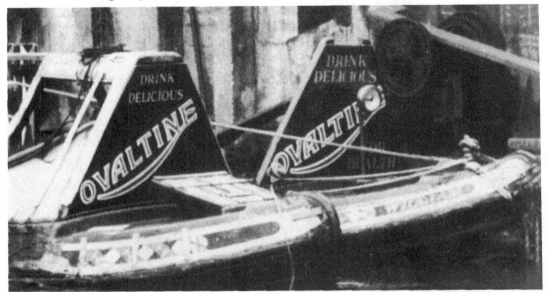

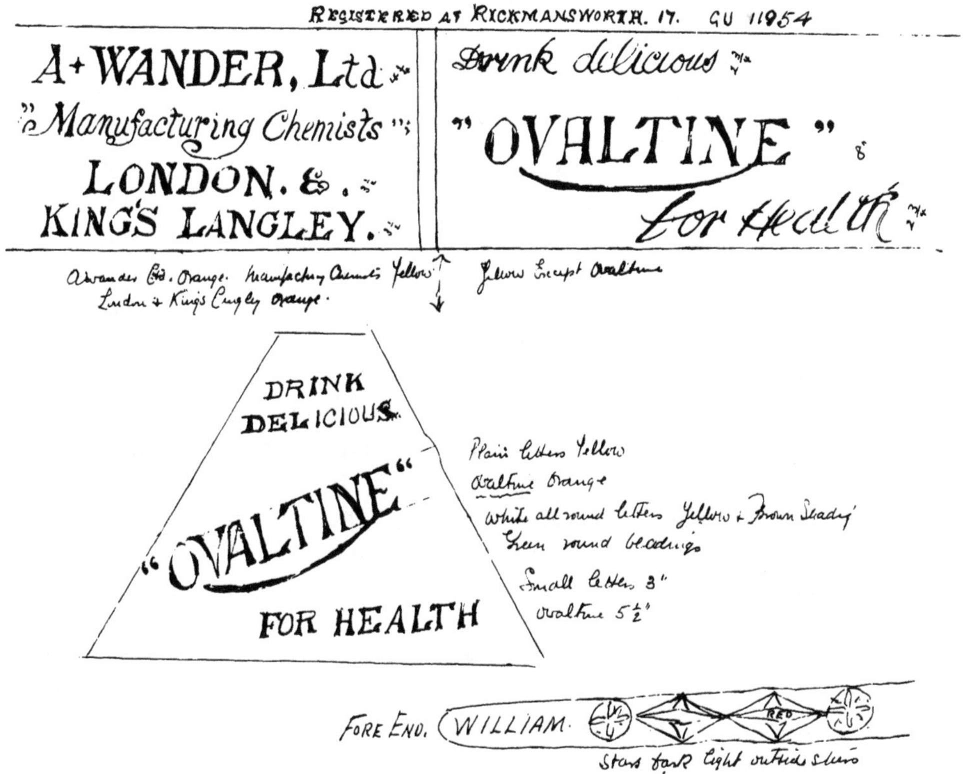

Fig. 11 *Dockyard notes on the painting and signwriting specification for an Ovaltine boat from Nurser Bros. dock at Braunston.*

The efforts of the reformer George Smith resulted in the passing of the two Canal Boats Acts of 1877 and 1884, which among other provisions, stipulated that every adult living aboard a boat should have at least 60 cu ft of free air space in the cabin, and that every child under twelve years old should have 40 cu ft. As the total capacity of the average boat cabin is a little over 200 cu ft, the legal effect was to limit the crew to a married couple, with up to two children. This gave rise to problems for the larger families and increased the practice of building a small cabin at the bows to allow two more children to be legally accommodated. An extra cabin at the front in place of the foredeck meant that the boat lost only a foot or two of stowage space in the hold. An extension of the stern cabin would have taken up valuable cargo space and increased the difficulty of loading the boat level, for a single large cabin would have concentrated buoyancy at one end.

The sides of the resulting fore-cabin are very low, only rising 12 to 18 in above the level of the top plank of the hull, and they camber in sharply. The cratch now sits along the after edge of the forecabin with the usual arrangement of deck-cloth. The cabin is painted in much the same style as the stern cabin, which will be dealt with fully later, except that the centre panels, which on the stern cabin usually carry the firm's name, are here left blank as they are so small, or sometimes simply bear the boat's name. In other respects, they are given the same treatments and colour schemes as the main living cabins.

The walking planks are supported by the cratch and at equidistant intervals by the mast and two identical stands, and finish on a block of wood on the forward edge of the stern cabin. The mast is built in the form of an upright box, the upper end open, into which a solid extension fits. This can be retracted into the box mast so that the top is just a few inches above the level of the planks, whose ends are notched to fit around it, or can be extended upwards and held in place by an iron pin to give an extra 3 ft or so of height. It is from the top of this mast that the horse tows, the height

14 *Fore cabins on Fellows, Morton & Clayton boats, tied up at Braunston during a strike in the early 1920s, and before their change from a mainly black and white livery to red, yellow and green.*

15 *Very fancy treatment of the fore cabin of a wide boat at Brentford during the 1930s.*

keeping the towline out of the water and clear of obstacles along the towpath.

The boxmast invariably has a design of diamonds on each of the four sides above the level of the beam that supports it, and thus above all but the bulkiest of loads. In its simplest form the design is of diagonals drawn from corner to corner on each side and the resulting triangles painted in four contrasting colours, two dark and two light, with sometimes a band of a fifth colour down each side. A final clarity is given to the whole structure by painting the iron bands around the mast black, and perhaps running a thin black line between the other colours. The top mast is usually plain red but may have a pattern of diamonds upon it. By the nature of its job, the constant rubbing as it is retracted causes the paintwork to suffer.

A very similar technique is used on the stands. These are upright planks tapering downwards, slotted through another crossbeam

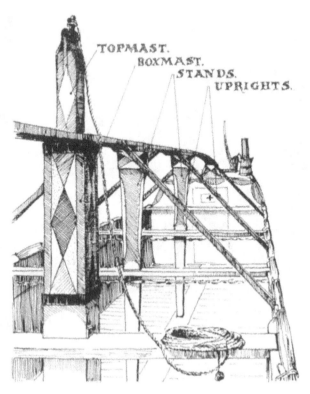

TOPMAST.
BOXMAST.
STANDS.
UPRIGHTS.

Fig. 12 *The separate parts of the framework supporting the gangplanks, which act as the ridgepole for the canvas top covers.*

at gunwale level and seated in a notch in the keelson. The top of the stand is strengthened by fixing small cross-pieces to each side and it is on these that the diagonal design appears again. The top half of the stand above the beam is painted a dark colour, usually blue or green, and the edges are chamfered in a style reminiscent of farm carts and picked out in contrasting yellow or white. The main surfaces of both forward and stern facing stands are regularly subdivided into a pattern of diamonds varying in complexity from two or three large central lozenges to a positive plaid of diagonals. More rarely they support a group of flowers or a compass wheel design, but the wear of constant

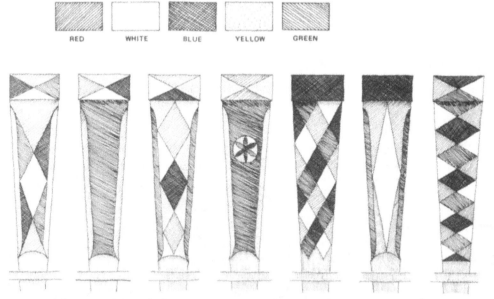

Fig. 13 *Some of the many patterns of diamonds that have been used on the stands usually with a matching design on the box-mast. The second from the left is the most common design.*

removal and replacement usually ensured a more easily repairable décor.

In the intervals between cratch, masts and stands, the planks are supported by 'uprights' which, despite their name, are pairs of wooden supports jammed diagonally between the gunwale and lower side of the planks. They are plain except for the forward pair between the cratch and mast, which stay in position, and thus in view, even when the boat is empty, and often have the ubiquitous diamonds running their full length. The firm of Cowburn & Cowpar ran several boats without any canvas covers at all, carrying acid carboys and similar imperishable goods and these boats were fitted with slightly-curved and well-decorated uprights for the full length of the hold, but this is exceptional.

The sternmost support of the planks is the 'cabin-block' on the

16 *Attractive diamond decoration on fore end, mast and stands on Midland & Coast Carrying Co boats at Old Hill dock.*

front edge of the cabin, and it is here that the more delicate, and possibly more feminine, approach to decoration is first shown insistently. The block itself is, on a horseboat or butty, about 9 in high, 2 in thick and increases in width downwards from the size of the walking plank to give it a firm seating on the forward edge of the cabin below. The four outside corners are chamfered strongly, giving the front and rear surfaces a concave outline and continuing the farm cart quality noted on the stands. The forward-facing side might be left blank, but the side facing astern, in full view of the steerer all the time, is always decorated with a motif. By far the most usual is a castle, closely followed by a design similar to that on the cabin slides, a circle in red, say, with green-scalloped border or similar, but any of the narrow boat

17 (above)   *A beautiful example of a well decorated boat, photographed in the Cannock coalfields; of especial interest is the young man painted on the cabin block, an unusual departure from roses and castles.*

18 (right)   *Detail of photograph 17.*

conventions might be made use of here – diamonds, diagonals or again, a bunch of roses.

It also appears to be the favourite ground for the deviationist. Several times I have heard of the famous sailor's head on the Players' cigarette packet being copied on to it, once of another advertising symbol incorporating a horse's head, and once of a copy of the 'stag at bay'. Because of its prominent position it both had pride of place and was testing ground for new ideas. If the boatman could bear to live with it for a few weeks and look at it daily without finding it unbearable, it was a good idea. The first few feet of the gangplank forward of the cabin-block might also have a design of diamonds, which show to advantage when the end of the topcloths are folded forward to ventilate the hold.

III   THE CABIN ROOF

The roof of the living cabin serves several supplementary purposes to the main one of keeping the rain out. It is an extension of the confined living space and serves as storage space for the water cans and mop as well as more specifically boating equipment – the short boathook, tiller and various ropes. It is the lunchtime dining table when food is taken on the move, and the place where the baby is put out in the sun. Add to these uses the fact that it is constantly under the eyes of the boat-steerer standing in the cabin hatch and it is not so surprising that a high standard of cleanliness, tidiness and decoration makes itself felt. The scruffiest of boats usually has the cabin roof neat and mopped clean.

The water cans are kept on the port side just forward of the chimney, where they are accessible by standing in the slide and reaching around the chimney. This is their traditional situation, and being constantly in the public eye as well as the boatman's, they are invariably painted with flowers, however sparse the decoration may be on the rest of the boat. The cans are made to a traditional pattern that dates back to early canal days, tapering slightly in shape, like an upturned bucket, with a small spout and a handle over the top. A strengthening band encircles it around

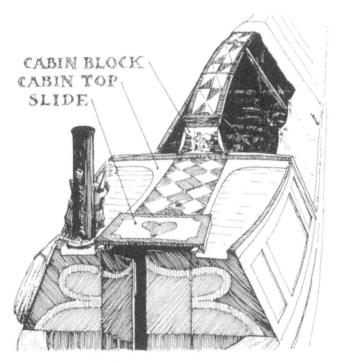

CABIN BLOCK
CABIN TOP
SLIDE

Fig. 14 *The layout of the stern cabin roof. The curving design shown on the cabin top is a regional variation seen on the boats of customers of the Anderton Company dock at Stoke-on-Trent, like Potter & Sons, and Henry Seddons & Sons.*

the middle, either as an added collar, or as grooves rolled into the main metal of the can. This carries, when the can is decorated, the most obvious concession to the public eye; proclaiming the name of the owner – the boatman's rather than the company's – for the world to see. As the world in this case consists largely of people he knows or who are illiterate, the proud name is a more flamboyant gesture than at first appears. Other mottoes appeared on this band in a similar mood – 'Staff of Life', 'Good luck', while one or two were unpleasantly smug – 'Buy your own cherries', loosely translated perhaps as 'I'm all right Jack'. The boatman's

Fig. 15 *Cabin sliding hatch, or 'slide', designs. Few had any special allegiance to one firm.*

own name was the most popular, however, and the longest-lived judging by the reference to Thomas Randle's can in *Household Words* in 1858 (Appendix 1).

The remainder of the can is smothered in roses. Each panel formed by the tinsmith's seams and beaded edges has a group of flowers, and castle scenes appear in the larger panels around the lower half of the can. With borders of diagonal stripes or a band of diamonds, a well-painted can presents a very rich appearance and is probably the most pattern-packed piece of equipment on the boat. If the water can is considered in isolation, the strong family resemblance to the Pennsylvanian Dutch-painted tinware is noticeable through to the finishing touches of lining out the whole object with thin cream or yellow lines.

The mop, standard narrow boat equipment, is kept forward of the can with its handle usually resting on the handle of the water can, or through it. The mops are homemade for the job out of thick rags which makes them easier to 'twizzle', the boatman's method of wringing them out by rolling the handle between the arms fast enough to spin the excess water out from the head. The favourite design is of barber's pole stripes running the full length of the handle in four or five colours, which looks even more interesting in the process of being twizzled. On the other side of the roof, handy to the boatman's right hand, lies the cabin shaft or short boathook, simply painted in one or two colours, or left as bare wood.

The usual ordinary base colour for the roof is plain red oxide. Bright red gloss paint is more often used on motor boats where the nonslip quality is less important than on a butty or horse boat where the roof has to be walked on to a greater extent. Probably the best treatment for appearance alone is to have the roof grained with a light oak or cedar wood graining scumble, in the same way as the interior furnishings of the cabin. Further decoration to the roof is usually a broad band of diamonds that runs centrally the length of the cabin, from slide right forward to the cabin-block, a purely aesthetic continuation of the line of the top planks. On motorboats this pattern usually extends from the slide only as far forward as the 'pigeon box', a small hatch or skylight in the engine room roof. It is finished off with an inch-wide line down each side, probably yellow against a red roof, or green or blue on a grained background. This again, with care in arranging the colour of the diamonds, continues the policy of abutting dark colours against light ones wherever possible – a regular rule, though flexible.

The painting of the pigeon box follows no set rule, with all the various possibilities being used at some time. The early motorboats were fitted with a simple, flat wooden box, like an upturned tray, that merely served to keep out the weather. This was treated in the same manner as the slides, a playing card motif or a circle, perhaps, simply outlined. A little later it seems that skylight and ventilator types with a pitched roof were introduced, and the two sides presented themselves as ideal grounds for a bunch of roses. The most common layout for the painting of a pigeon box is basically green, with a group of flowers on the hinged lids each side, a castle panel at each end (particularly that facing astern), and a line of diamonds on the central ridge.

It provides an interesting example of a visibly changing boat tradition. Pigeon boxes are, by their motor boat nature, only recent innovations on narrow boats, but from their fairly humble beginnings they developed to a very important part of the boats' furnishings, regularly fitted with brass portholes and providing a base for several large brass ornaments, as well as painted additions. Bear in mind that they are easily detachable and interchangeable, staying with the owners even when they change boats, and it is more understandable why such care is lavished on these particular pieces of equipment. As they are regularly the private property of the boatman, they more often bear the

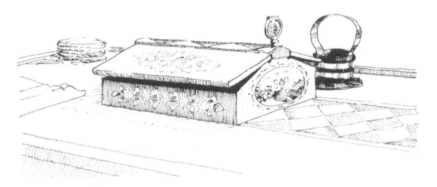

Fig. 16 *A motor boat's decorated 'pigeon box' or engine room ventilator, complete with a little swinging horse-brass ornament.*

painted work of the boatman himself than that of the last dockyard at which the boat was docked.

IV THE BACK OF THE CABIN

The misleadingly simple curving design that appears without fail on the closed back doors of the narrow boat is an interesting problem, without an obvious origin. In its simplest form it merely echoes the outline of the rear elevation of the cabin, but instead of a sharp corner echoing the junction of the cabin sides with the roof, the line of the design curves gently to change direction, and continues until it rises to a point in the middle, on the cabin doors' opening line. This design is not the result of any constructional method, as the panelling of the cabin sides might be, and it is not a 'simple' in the sense of 'naive' design, as the diamond patterns that appear everywhere else are. It does not follow any easy formula for the shape that it occupies and yet, with all its variations, it does follow a distinct convention, one to which I can find no parallel in any nautical way.

There is, however, one area of transport where a very similar design appears, although with no obvious connection with narrow boats. Certain regional types of heavy farm waggons have on the front board of the waggon body a painted shape that has become

19 *There was a close connection between horse drawn road haulage and canal steerage and the main paintwork has as much to do with carts and waggons as it does with ships and the sea. Note the water barrel in use on the most distant boat in this picture taken at Castlefield, Manchester.*

known as the 'spectacles', due to the obvious resemblance. Mr C. F. Tebbutt FSA made an interesting study of this design and published an article on his results in *Man* in August 1955. In this he traces the pattern back to the importation of the Scotch cart, a lighter farm vehicle than the English waggon. These had been made in a similar style and painted with the 'spectacles' trade mark since the early nineteenth century, but Mr Tebbutt could not trace the pattern before this. The interesting thing is that as these

Fig. 17 *A comparison between the narrow boat designs in the left-hand column with the farm cart designs in the right-hand one makes a connection or a common origin seem quite possible.*

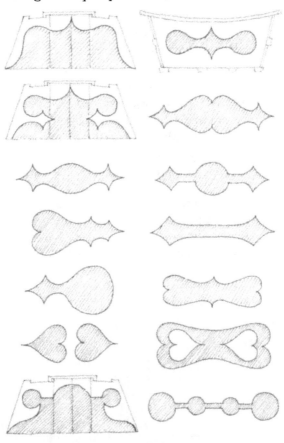

vehicles were exported from Scotland, the local wheelwrights gradually took over their manufacture and style. The 'spectacle' design not only stayed, but developed into many regional variations, particularly in Ireland, where the Scotch cart became very popular. The commonest design on the back of a boat cabin exactly resembles half the usual 'spectacles', while the developments that appear on coal boats of the Black Country bear a closer resemblance to the complete farm waggon designs of the English wainwrights. This resemblance alone could barely be called evidence, but if this possible origin is kept in mind one begins to think that other rather obscure shapes that appear on narrow boats could have come from the same stable. The shape that used to appear on the forward top bends of Fellows, Morton & Clayton's boats and on the engine room slides, and the design on the sides of the rudder stock of their horse boats seem to have the same root, while the chamfering on the stands, cabin-block and butty tiller hark back to the essential weight-saving of wooden road and farm vehicles.

Mr Tebbutt also found that in Donegal the carts had playing-card suit designs – 'diamonds, hearts, spades or clubs on the front in that order of frequency. The club always had its shaft turned to the left, and so might represent a shamrock'. Here we have some facts that point to a possible connection with narrow boats; diamonds, hearts and clubs with the same one-way tail appear throughout the canal system as the favoured designs on cabin slides, deck lids and cabin-blocks, although the use of the spade is more rare.

The original construction of this design on the Scotch cart, and on the later English waggons, was by cutting out the shape in the top layer of tongued and grooved boards revealing the second layer below, which were painted in a contrasting colour. The sawn edges were bevelled and painted, resulting in an outline to the shape much as the boat shape is usually outlined by an inch-wide yellow line between the colours. However, the 'constructed' spectacles quite soon became merely a painted trademark, and thus offered itself as an easily copied design. If

Key to Colour Representation

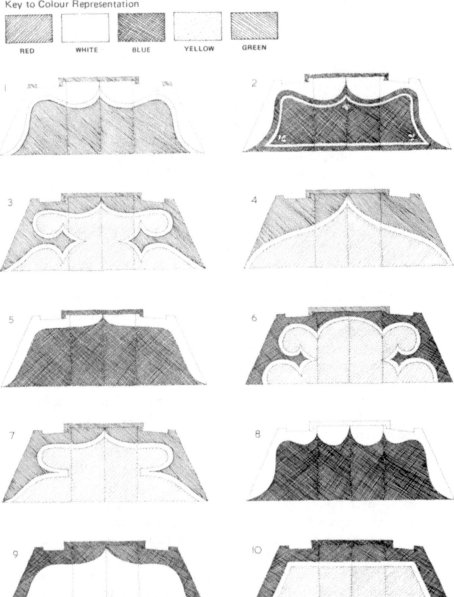

RED WHITE BLUE YELLOW GREEN

there is any connection it could have come about in two ways; either the influence of the design was felt from Lincolnshire and the Fens where the 'spectacles' were standard farm waggon decorations, or it suggests an Irish influence, particularly in conjunction with the playing-card motifs. I must leave further conjecture for further evidence.

The colours in which the boat design is carried out are usually two of the darker colours, red and green for example, separated by a white or yellow line. The outer or upper of the two colours is sometimes the same as that of the surrounding boards of the cabin side, or outer border, and the effect is to disguise the proper outline of the back of the cabin. The use of the scalloped border of the cabin slides, the chamfering on cabin-block and stands, as well as this back door design, achieve this same effect. Perhaps the subconscious purpose of some of these shapes and strong contrasts is to disguise and enrich the harsh utilitarian outlines of the boats, in rather the same way that dazzle camouflage paintwork of first world war shipping was intended to make details more difficult to see, and thus the ship more difficult to identify. Similar treatment is often given to the front of the cabin, facing into the hold, by painting black scallops round the edge against the common red bulkhead, a widespread design that appears to be a boatman's innovation rather than one company's livery.

Fig. 18 (opposite) *The design that always appears on the back of the cabin has a lot of variations though they all seem to stem from a common root. This diagram is from photographs of boats of the following companies: 1) Fellows, Morton & Clayton's pattern, the one preferred by the majority of companies, 2) a slightly different treatment of the same shape on British Transport Waterways boats, just after nationalisation, 3) the most common variation, 4) Jon. Horsefield Ltd, Runcorn, 5) Severn & Canal Carrying Co, 6) Ovaltines, Kings Langley, 7) Anderton Company dock customers, 8) Associated Canal Carriers Ltd, Northampton, 9) Shropshire Union Railway & Canal Co, 10) The Grand Union Carrying Co's attempt at rationalisation in the 1930s.*

Fig. 19 *World War I 'dazzle' camouflage. By confusing the ship's outlines, its speed, direction and real character were made more difficult to ascertain.*

V   THE CABIN SIDES

The sides of the stern cabin of a narrow boat are the ultimate pride of the boat, proclaiming the ownership in bold lettering. Steam and motor boats have their names there and all have in smaller official lettering the various numbers that the boat has been allotted for purposes of cabin registration, canal tolls and individual fleet numbers; but at the same moment of being part of the glory of a boat, they are also the part that has least to do with the folk art aspects of narrow boat decoration. Regardless of the fact that they may be the most beautiful examples of the signwriter's art, colourful and well composed, they are essentially developments of canal company bye-laws and regulations. As an example, the regulations for the Grand Junction Canal in 1793 read

That every Owner, Master or Person having the Care or Command of any Boat, Barge or other Vessel, passing upon the said Canal shall cause his Name and Place of Abode, and the Number of his or her Boat, Barge or other Vessel, to be painted in Large White Capital Letters and Figures on a Black Ground, three inches high at the least and of a proportionable Breadth on the Outside of the Head or Stern of every such Boat . . . higher than the place to which the same shall sink into the Water when Full Laden

and nearly every other canal company required some such identification. Needless to say this requirement very soon became a reason or excuse for the firm of carriers to emblazon its name

20 *Harry Broadhead, a part-time signwriter, painting the registration number on Sophie Scragg's boat at Fellows, Morton & Clayton's Broad Street depot at Wolverhampton in 1947.*

21 *A boat acquired from the Shropshire Union Railways & Canal Company by one of their customers when they gave up carrying in 1921. Although the firm's name has changed, the colour scheme is only slightly altered from the SUR & C Co livery. Signwriting is by J. Harry Taylor except the boat's name which is carved into the top plank in the standard SU way.*

on the cabin side as the finest sort of advertisement. It also possibly explains the earlier preponderance of black and white colour schemes among the larger carriers.

The styles of lettering now associated with narrow boats are of an old fashioned kind with large serifs, heavily blocked in two colours or two tones to throw the letters into relief. The lettering has a decorative quality compared to modern practice that merges well with the overall texture of boat painting, although there is nothing specifically 'folk' about it. It is merely a hangover from the general style of signwriting used everywhere at one time, that has found a perfect setting, and has assumed a quality of having been there forever by its very rightness.

The most popular lettering, particularly among the owner-boatman and the smaller companies is an Egyptian style, or one called generically Ionic. The Victorian term 'Egyptian' refers to roman-based lettering where the serif is formed with a solid square ending block, giving it a heavy architectural weight which

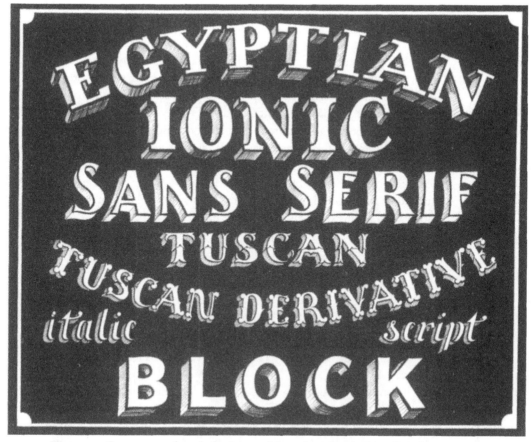

Fig. 20 *Some examples of the favoured boat lettering styles referred to in the text.*

presumably led to its name, while 'Ionic' refers to an intermediate form where the main strokes of the letter curve out to meet the smaller square ended serif. The illustration should clarify this. Standard roman lettering with its pointed serifs is surprisingly scarce even in its more extreme 'bold' forms. The only roman characteristic consistently used is the clear contrast between thick strokes and thin strokes.

Following these in popularity is the signwriters' sans serif. In this the serif is merely suggested by a thickening at the end of each stroke, a style that can be done with a sort of handwriting ease by a practising signwriter. It is a comparatively easy letter to write with a brush, as the concave sides of each stroke of the letter allow a certain flexibility in size and direction, intentional or otherwise, to pass less noticeably. For pure patterned effect the knotty lettering favoured by some northern companies and dockyards must take first place. It is derived from 'Tuscan' lettering where the ends of the letter strokes bifurcate to give leaflike pointed serifs, but in the nameless boat lettering the serifs turn out into round protuberances giving any block of writing done with it an extremely decorative texture.

After these favourites, almost any lettering derived from the standard alphabet is to be met with somewhere. Simple block lettering would seem to work against the decorative principle, but the use made of it on Thomas Clayton's boats with the associated block projection painted in two tones achieves a proud 'in keeping' effect. An oddity on the Thomas Clayton horse boats is the use of Old English or black letter on the fleet number panel of the cabin side, the only example I have discovered for this style on canal boats.

The smaller lettering on the cabin sides, the adjectival phrases such as 'Coal Factors' or 'Canal Steerage', and on occasions, the firm's address, is usually in a simple script with perhaps an added flourish to the capitals.

The name of the horse boat or butty is invariably painted on

22 *This tar tanker, photographed in Wolverhampton locks in 1965, makes attractive use of very simple lettering. Decoration and signwriting are by Fred Winnet at Thos Clayton's own dock at Oldbury.*

23 *The boat's name carved into the stern plank of an ex-Shropshire Union boat, still in good heart when photographed in 1973.*

the top strake at the stern and uses the same lettering styles already mentioned, upper case, very often italic, blocked out in contrasting colours. Certain companies had the boat's name cut in the wood of the top plank, although this followed letter-cutting practice rather than signwriting, and was Bold Roman in style with the strokes finishing with sharp pointed serifs, and was picked out in black against a plain white background. This simple and elegant name-cutting was probably more common in the last century, and was only ousted by a preference for a more decorative approach latterly. This certainly happened with the Anderton Company whose predominantly black and white livery changed to a more colourful style just before the last war, although their own dockyard was already renowned for fine decorative paintwork on other firm's boats.

The overall design of the cabin side is often finished with painted scroll work. This is interesting in that this baroque touch occurs only in conjunction with the signwriter's work and never among the many other patterns of the boat. Scrollwork was seen at its boldest and most complicated on the steam and early motor boats which suggests that it is an example of one of the most recent developments of the tradition. Here again Fellows, Morton & Clayton seem to have been the originators, but the use of scroll work obviously appealed to the hauliers of the Black Country,

73

24 *The year is 1932, and the pride taken in the power of motor boats is obvious in the flamboyant display of scroll work on this one belonging to the forerunners of the Grand Union Canal Carrying Company.*

where the coal boat tugs are enriched almost solely by splendid scrolls. The resulting impression gained from both tugs and steamers is one of tremendous pride and power, contrasting with the more houseproud and delicate effect of the family horse boat.

The main background colours of the lettered panels do not conform so rigidly to the primary group carried out in other boat designs. Ignoring the larger companies' earlier preference for black, the usual colour is a medium or dark tone, red or green, but considerable use was made of maroon and chocolate as well as very dark greens and blues. It follows that the lettering is always light in tone, white or cream, to contrast. The blocking or three-dimensional appearance is painted in two tones or colours contrasting with background and lettering, this third colour giving the cabin side its characteristic richness. Smaller lettering and scroll work is treated in the same way.

From the conclusion that the cabin side lettering and its advertising uses were more the taste of the boat owner than the boatman, one would not expect the domestic and folk art designs of roses and castles to appear there. This may have been true except for a notable group exception, the 'number ones' or owner boatmen. The only thing they felt it necessary to advertise was their standing in boat society so the cabin sides, although displaying their names also displayed the decorative standards they had reached in the rivalry for the most glorious boat. The moulding edging the cabin-side panels was echoed further by more intricate borders, and the panels filled with bunches of flowers and castles as well as the lettering. They began to set a different standard of decoration by regarding the whole boat as a ground for paintings, and by treating the cabin panels with the same domestic respect as the inside of the cabins.

Following the introduction of roses to the cabin sides, boatmen of some of the larger firms prevailed upon their bosses to have them introduced into the company livery and they became more widespread, gradually ousting scroll work in popularity. From photographic evidence this process seems to have accelerated during the 1930s; firms like Samuel Barlow and Faulkner, both renowned for their paintwork, had scrolls on cabin-sides where roses appear later and the Anderton Company as previously noted accepted the boatman's favourite motifs as standard just before World War II. The majority of the carriers' boats, however, remained with purely lettered panels.

The cabin side of a horse boat is divided, for no constructional reason, into two or three recessed panels by wooden framing, three or four inches wide with a decorative wooden moulding at the edges. There is a large main one bearing the firm's name,

25 *The rich quality that deep blocking out gives to fairly simple sans serif lettering can be seen on this cabin side, the work of Nurser Bros dock during the thirties.*

26 *Boats ascending Runcorn locks about 1910, an interesting contrast between the well decorated* Scotia *behind to the rather austere paintwork of the Anderton Company boat in front.*

a smaller one astern of it, with sometimes a smaller one ahead as well. They were usually used for official lettering purposes, fleet numbers and the Canal Boats Act registration number, but again it seems that the owner boatmen set the fashion for a more colourful use by treating them as grounds for landscapes. It is obviously an old idea as the picture illustrating *Life on the Upper Thames* in 1873 shows the sternmost panel used for a castle landscape very well. Fellows, Morton & Clayton kept this panel for lettering until the end, but others changed to the more artistic approach in the same way as they did with the lettering panel. A photograph of Faulkner's boats in 1913 shows it used for official lettering while a picture taken in the 1920s shows a castle occupying the same space; in this case the whole livery has changed from black and white to a more colourful scheme with the panel framing oak

Plate V (Above):   *Two stages in the work of Ron Hough; he was taught in his craft by Frank Nurser of Braunston Dock, and continues to work at Braunston.* (Below):   *A group of roses by another Nurser pupil Dennis Clark of Rugby.*

Plates VI and VII *Castles by different painters which despite individual detail have a unity of style which only appears on the English canals.*
(Opposite): *A decorative panel painted by Frank Jones of Leighton Buzzard.*

(Below): *Part of a Cowburn & Cowpar cabin by Isaiah Atkins of Polesworth dock.*

Plate VIII (Above): *Combinations of canal boat lettering with traditional decoration by Herbert Tooley of Banbury. (Below): A cabin block by Frank Nurser for one of Chas. Nelson & Company's boats, which had the cockerel as a trade mark.*

27 *A well decorated motor boat photographed at Yarwoods about 1936. Signwriting by David Dykes, decoration by George Preston.*

grained. In the south the registration town and number was very often signwritten along the top of the cabin side on the framing, but many northern firms used one of the smaller panels for this purpose. The Mersey-Weaver Company's boats had the sternmost panel painted in an unusual way with a large simple eight-petalled star or flower design. This is sometimes referred to as the 'Seddon's Star' so it is likely that it formed part of Henry Seddon's boat decoration at some point. It could, however, be derived from a town's registration mark. Boats registered as Runcorn for example often had the number marked alongside or within a Star of David, whilst boats registered at Chester had a small wheatsheaf after the number.

The cabinside layout of motor boats is rather different, and it was rare to have castles on a motor boat. Exceptions are again the number one's boats like John Wilson's *Mabel* which was a converted horse boat and continued his previous style, and a few larger firms like Cowburn & Cowpar of Manchester who had their motor boats built with a castle panel astern. The main panel of the cabin side bore, of course, the firm's name, with the name of the boat on the side of the engine room, forward of the living cabin. The lettering is usually set up on a curve with the panel finished with scrolls or bunches of flowers. Several firms like the Severn & Canal Carrying Company never named their motor boats but merely had 'Motor Boat No 5', or whichever number it was, under the firm's name on the larger cabin side panel.

VI   THE RUDDER AND TILLER

The oil painting of Pickford's boat *Hope* of about 1820 in the Museum of British Transport, and a model made in 1873, in Dudley Museum collection, agree in showing the rudder simply painted with wide horizontal bands of colour, and this would seem to have been common. During the last few years, an almost standard design has developed that is best described by cross-reference to the illustration showing a Samuel Barlow Company rudder. This has the effect of large areas of colour with a touch of white here and there, whereas earlier examples appear to have been painted white with added coloured shapes and symbols as decoration. As the majority of the larger carriers had a basically black and white colour scheme, this seems a likely development, and puts some order into the later patterns.

The top of the main rudder stock, which is rounded over its thickness, always has a circle painted on it, usually blue; as it is painted on the curved surface, like laying a pancake over it, the resulting shape on each side is a downward-carrying semicircle. The 'dazzle-disguise' effect of this is to give a dished or scalloped appearance to the top of the rudder. Similar treatment is given to the bracket at the back, where the main blade of the rudder joins the stock. Here the colour usually finishes with a varying number of scallop shapes, reminiscent of farm cart chamfering.

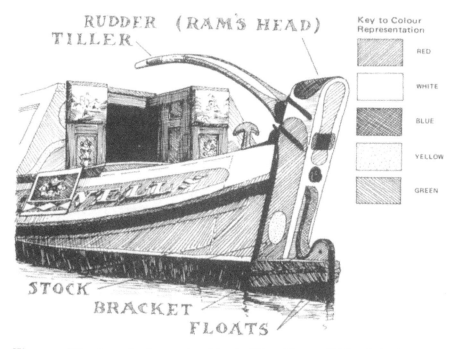

RUDDER (RAM'S HEAD)
TILLER

Key to Colour
Representation

RED
WHITE
BLUE
YELLOW
GREEN

STOCK
BRACKET
FLOATS

Fig. 21 *The stern of a boat painted in the Thos Clayton (Oldbury) Ltd colour scheme. The decorated canvas flap is to keep the scrubbed wooden capping pieces clean.*

Another usual feature is the dark toned colour of the 'floats', the pieces of wood that connect the top of the boards of the rudder blade to the stock. They rarely have any further decoration beyond picking out the guard iron in black. The same colour, continuing up the forward chamfers of the stock against the majority white, certainly does relieve the squareness and improves the elegance.

After these common features the variations begin in earnest. The sides of the stock present the main areas for design and most popular latterly is a red section or shape from the floats extending toward the blue rounded at the top. In the north this tends to occupy the centre of the available space, leaving an equidistant border of white all around it, the resulting shape being the sole design. In the south, however, the red generally covers the whole of the side of the stock, giving a wide enough area of colour to act as a background for further decoration. In both cases the red is finished at the top in a convex semicircle opposing the blue disc curving down.

Probably the commonest symbol used on the side of the rudder is the little six-petalled 'compass wheel', very attractive although very simple to set out with a pair of compasses. On a dark background the larger areas are light with the 'spokes' dark to

Fig. 22 *A selection of rudders: 1) Samuel Barlow Coal Co, 2) from an 1873 model in the Black Country Museum's collection, 3) Fellows, Morton & Clayton Ltd about 1900, 4) J. E. Southern & Co Manchester, 5) Mersey, Weaver & Ship Canal Carrying Co, 6) John Walley, Stoke-on-Trent, 7) A. & A. Peate, Oswestry, 8) Mr Beech of Acton Bridge. Numbers 3, 6, 7, 8 are from black and white photographs, so the colours indicated by the shading have been judged from the tone they appear.*

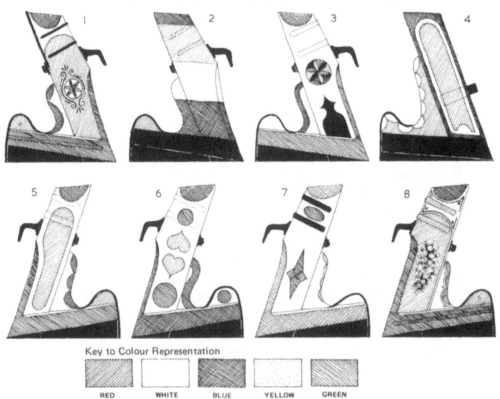

Key to Colour Representation

RED   WHITE   BLUE   YELLOW   GREEN

contrast, and vice versa on a light ground. It appears on a Fellows, Morton & Clayton boat in a photograph of 1900 and has been in common use in this century. The standard Fellows, Morton & Clayton rudder insignia is a strange little shape that defies a simple written description, and is one of those designs that seem to owe allegiance to farm carts more than anything else. It was marked in black on the white stock until the change in colour scheme in the 1920s, after which it continued in red.

Not unexpectedly the owner-boatmen evolved the most decorative treatment and used the sides of the rudder as grounds for groups of flowers as well as the popular compass wheel. The red triangle painted on the hull between the guard and the loaded water line might have been a number one's innovation. It continues the line of the floats and the colour mass of the side of the rudder, accentuating the rise to the stern post and forming yet another background for roses.

Roses occasionally occupy the sides of the tiller, or many small diamonds on four of the eight faces, with stripes of colour separating them on the remaining four. Simpler, but very effective, is to paint the surfaces to contrast with one another for their full length, ending in a few vertical bands towards the handgrip. It is a little surprising, considering the tiller's tapering chamfered shape, that the commonest style is merely to paint it in thirds of its length in three colours. The same pattern transferred to many motor boats, although the favourite design with the boatmen was undoubtedly the barber's pole stripe, twirling up the rudder and along the detachable tiller in one continuous flow. This works best when carried out in four colours, two light ones alternating with two dark ones, such as white – red – yellow – blue, and back to white. If three or five colours are used the similarly toned ones tend to merge at a distance to give a broad dark band against a thin light one, or vice versa, losing some of the clarity and symmetry of the design.

Enquiries about the technique of setting out the stripes usually receive comments about a tin of striped paint, or spinning with one hand, while painting down the length with the other! In practice four pieces of cotton is the more mundane truth. After carefully winding them equally spaced around the object, two of the colours can be painted in, the cotton removed, and the other two painted neatly when the first colours are dry. Some painters do it freehand but it is difficult to avoid altering the proportions of the stripes as the work proceeds. It is not a widely used design, only being strictly normal on mop handle and motor boat tillers. It appears on the butty tiller at times, on the whip handle, and on the bobbins and swingle tree or spreader of a well-painted horse harness set. There is a related design used on the tinware where the bottom rim of the water can, handbowl, and horse's feed tin is decorated with diagonal stripes, but because of its narrowness, it appears as a line of sloping rectangles rather than as barber's pole stripes.

VII   THE STERN

All motor boat sterns are painted in much the same way, dictated partly by their shape, and partly by practical considerations. The large semi-circular counterblock to which the side planking of

28   Alice *was converted to a motor boat and maintained by the Anderton Company dock, and was decorated by their painter William Hodgson. Note his unusual patterns round the counter in this photograph, taken in 1950.*

a wooden boat is fixed is protected by 'D' section guard iron at top and bottom, with one or two intermediate ones. The areas between these guards are painted in plain colours, forward to where the boat approaches its maximum beam. This point roughly coincides with the back of the cabin, where it is usual to finish the colours in concave curves, just aft of where the rainwater drains off the counter deck. The same pattern of guard irons prevails on the iron and steel boats, giving extra rigidity to the counter where the butty unavoidably runs up and bumps the motor in various manoeuvres, another reason why the more fancy techniques are not lavished around the stern. The commonest colour scheme is to paint the top space, usually the largest, white, perhaps for visibility to other boats, and the space below red. A third might be green or blue, with the intervening guards painted black to contrast.

The stern of the horse boat or butty, however, has to satisfy a rather different set of considerations. The top planks are the invariable positions for the boat's name, they are close to the cabin, practically the front door step, and being at the back of the boat, are less liable to normal rubbing and wear; not surprisingly then, they get the full decorative treatment. The majority of boats have a dark centre section to act as a contrasting background to the lettering, bordered by a white line, in the same way as the fore end is treated. This is the same style as on the boats of the 1820s, as can be seen in Shepherd's engravings and the *Hope* painting. Some companies have austere white planks, with the name as the only motif on them, but most use heavily blocked and serifed lettering on a red base and achieve a rich effect. Although using the central portion for the name removes the possibility of using it for any other subdividing patterns, the decoration often continues for a much greater distance along the plank than the corresponding paintwork of the fore end, in extreme cases the full length of the cabin. The light border continues, and unifies the design of crescents, compass wheels, diamonds, and the occasional bunch of roses which make up the extension of the name panel astern.

29 *This butty is rather unusual in making so much use of scrolls in its decoration; a fine piece of signwriting, taken at Lostock Gralam before World War II.*

VIII   THE CABIN INTERIOR

It is difficult to realise just how small a boat cabin is until the measurements are written down, and one considers a complete family being reared in it. The basic and necessary utensils and clothes would seem to fill a cupboard of a similar size. It is seldom longer than 9 ft and very often much less. This measurement is from inside the entrance, which faces astern, to the bulkhead door that, in the butty boat leads forward into the cargo hold, and in the motor boat into the engine room. The overall width of the boat cannot exceed 7 ft by more than an inch or so, and the effective width inside is nearer 6 ft. A few boats give standing headroom of 6 ft in the cabin, but the majority are much lower. Within these boundaries is built a masterpiece of space utilisation, in essentials the same as it was a hundred years ago.

The entrance consists of a pair of doors that open outwards into a little cockpit on a horse boat, or to the stern deck on a motor boat. Directly inside on the left, that is on the port side, is the spiritual centre of the cabin, the stove or cooking range. Next to this is a floor to ceiling cupboard at a slight angle to the wall. The door to the top half of this cupboard hinges out and down to form a table and is known, sensibly, as the 'table-cupboard'. Below this is a shallow cutlery drawer, with a small cupboard below that again. Beyond is another cupboard continuing forward to the bulkhead. The topmost section is for clothes while the central part houses mattress and bedding. The door to this part also folds out and down to form a bridge with the seat which runs along the right-hand side of the cabin. This bridge is the cross or main bed, generally about 3½ ft wide and able to be put up during the day to afford a clear passage through. Under the cross-bed and the 'side-bed' opposite are linen drawers, and yet another cupboard is built above the side-bed just inside the entrance doors on the right-hand side. The furnishings are completed with a little drawer close to the ceiling just inside the doors on the left. This is the 'ticket drawer' where all the lock

30 *Harold Hood, the last foreman at the Anderton Company dock, sitting on the side bed and retouching flowers on the cross bed flap. The overall graining of the cabin can be seen and the use of moulding and extra painted borders, and the way the table cupboard and the drawer below it are picked out in a contrasting green.*

31 *A group of flowers by an unknown painter on the top of the table cupboard flap, the piece of furniture most commonly decorated.*

passes and toll tickets are kept, ·convenient to the steerer. All this furniture is fairly simply built in soft wood, but much use is made of panelling and moulding to improve its looks. Cupboard doors and drawers are built with recessed central panels edged with mouldings, the larger areas of the walls are panelled, and narrow mouldings are used to edge all cupboards and every available corner.

The standard treatment is then to undercoat everything with a buff yellow colour, and to combgrain it with a light oak scumble – walls, cupboards, seats and ceiling. This achieves a number of objects that may or may not have been originally intended. It softens and darkens the whole cabin, optically blurring the edges, it disguises mistakes and bad surfaces, and it gives the whole structure an overall texture and cohesion. This may have been done originally with much skill and subtlety, but recent examples seen have been a little crudely done, although still meeting the above requirements. It may be that the standard has fallen as graining of any sort has gone out of fashion and the workmen out of practice, or it may be that both boatmen and boat builder positively like the repetitive design of heavy combed graining. It certainly looks well when varnished, with the mouldings picked out in red, and the odd cupboard door in green to contrast. The only limit to the amount of extra painted decoration in the cabin was the amount that the boatman could afford, as in most cases the inside decoration was at his private expense. The owner paid for the outside work, and for the cabin graining as he was bound to do in law, but extra fancy work inside the cabin was the captain's responsibility. He had to come to a private arrangement with the dock painter for this, or do it himself.

The cabin doors are built to a standard pattern, with a square panel at the top bearing a castle scene, a central recessed panel with flowers in it, and a lower panel usually left plain except perhaps for a little star pattern or scroll. Doors are invariably

32 *The cabin doors of the wide boat* Golden Spray *in Brentford lock, displaying the beautiful paintwork of Bushell Bros' dock at Tring.*

decorated somehow as they are open much of the time and something of a showpiece to the outside world. After the doors, the most usually painted part is the table-cupboard, which has a castle in the central panel and flowers at the top even in the most sparsely decorated cabin. Next in popularity are roses on the knife drawer and the ticket drawer, and a landscape on the forward bulkhead door. After that every cupboard door and drawer has equal importance, with the panels of the walls being possibly the ultimate in complete decoration. By the time the movable cabin equipment is decorated and moved in, like the handbowl, stool and seatboard, the effect is already pretty stunning.

The boatwoman, however, is not content with this and proceeds to hide much of the paintwork with pieces of white crotchet lace hung from every shelf and ledge. She then conceals much of that by hanging her collection of lace-edged souvenir plates against it and uses them as a background to family photographs and brass knick-knacks. She creates such an Aladdin's cave of intricate textures and patterns that it never occurs to the observer to consider how small the cabin really is. Its job is therefore done.

The cabin is part of the boatwoman's self-expression as well as her home; by its appearance and cleanliness she proclaims her self-respect and standing in the boat society, in the same way that a scrubbed front doorstep, polished door knocker, and clean lace curtains at the window are the outward signs of a respectable house in the town, signs to be read by the practised eyes of the neighbours. It is essential for any narrow boat to have the water can decorated, the brasswork polished and the fancy ropework scrubbed white; any standard lower than this suggests poverty and a lack of pride. Unique features of the boatwoman's home are its size and close relationship with her husband's job, and the way her standards have spread all over the boat to include the tools and practical equipment of canal boating.

33 (opposite) *The confusing intricacy of the patterns and textures in Fred and Rose Gibbs' cabin makes its small size of much less importance than its rich quality.*

CHAPTER 4

'Van-Dyking' and the Painters

Although it may seem to a modern business man extravagant to paint decorative pictures on canal boats at all – 'van-dyking' in boatman's slang – once the tradition had reached the point where no boat was regarded as complete until it was decorated, the owner dared not do without pictures entirely for fear of losing all his skilled crews. After accepting the minimum cost demanded by the boatman, the boat owner was just as interested in cutting costs as anyone else. With traditional painting techniques the customer has the maximum effect from a minimum of painter's effort and cost. Tommy Williams, a well-known dock owner and painter, even experimented with stencils for his castles during the 1930s, but with dull and geometrical results. Boat painters had to evolve a fairly foolproof technique that could guarantee success without artistic standing-back or time-wasting retouching. Whether they developed their own slick, speedy method or were handed on from elsewhere is difficult to tell, but all twentieth century canal-painting seems to stem from a common root.

I am convinced that the work of the dockyard painters is the backbone of the tradition's continuity of style. The majority learned their trade in the ordinary master/apprentice relationship and, being craftsmen rather than artists, they followed their master's way of painting and, excluding their personal improvements and touches, continued to work and teach that same basic style. It follows that their work holds clues to earlier styles if it were possible to sift the personal additions from the kernel inherited from the master painter. Unfortunately evidence does not go back very far, although the master/apprentice connection can be seen in much existing paintwork. The boatman painter,

34 *The graceful brushwork of a very professional painter can be seen in this handbowl by Frank Jones of Leighton Buzzard.*

too, usually follows the work of the dock painter with whom he had most contact and whose work is most familiar. Initially work will be a bad, slavish copy of the tradesman, but practice and confidence soon create a personal style still showing traditional characteristics even if of amateurish finish. Thus we must look again to the dock painter for a direct line back to its origin.

Techniques used are similar throughout the country, although individual styles are fairly easily recognisable within the convention. Some painters use a variety of flowers but the most important ones to us would be the stylised roses common to all. Equally, some painters use motifs other than a castle in the pictorial panels – dogs, churches or horses perhaps – but castles form the bulk of the work.

Under scrutiny, painting methods for flowers are fairly obvious and simple, surprisingly so in view of the decorative results. The first stage is to mark out roughly in chalk the flower pattern,

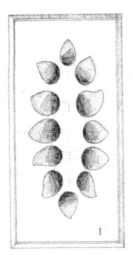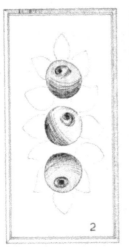

Fig. 23 *Four stages in painting a group of canal roses: 1) the leaves over a chalked layout, 2) a disc of background colour to each flower, 3) the 'petals', 4) the finishing touches, leaf veins, highlights and stamens.*

although the more confident would omit this. Then the leaves are painted to contrast with the background, with a black or dark brown shadow brushed into the wet green paint on the base edge nearest to the flowers. This gives a three-dimensional quality to the group and a darker contrast to the eventual flowers. A pointed leaf with a brown shadow is preferred in the south, while the north favours a rounded leaf and black shadow, with groups of intermediate budding leaves helping towards a very neat design. The spiky quality of the leaves is added later by painting in the veins and, in the north, with small flecks of white around the outer edges. The next stage is to paint round blobs of colour where the flowers are planned, to act as a background shape and colour upon which to work the flower petals. If the rose is to be red the background will be a roundel of black varying to a dark red-brown; where it is to be yellow, anything from a bright orange to a dirty yellow-brown, and where a white rose is required a background of pink or red is used. More accomplished painters brush a darker coloured heart into the shape while the paint is still wet, to help the appearance of depth. Colours of roses are invariably red, yellow or white, often arranged in groups with an equal number of each colour.

Some southern painters made much use of a mass of daisylike flowers with roses, usually consisting of many single brush stroke white petals on a blue base, although yellow, red and blue have been used. In the later Potteries style the equivalent extra flower is one like a small blue pansy, but both are the finishing touch rather than the main feature.

When the background colours are dry, or nearly so, the petals of the roses are painted in, and form the stage where individual styles differ most noticeably. Some use a large diagonal stroke with several smaller ones to complement it, while others have a central crescent representing the tight body of the rose, with a series of small strokes to suggest the opened petals curling away

35 *The canal flowers are seen at their most abstract on this stool by Fred Winnet. Each stage of the painting has been formalised to such an extent that the result is a neat, well-defined decorative pattern rather than a picture of flowers.*

36 *A panel by George Crowshaw showing daisy-like flowers as well as the formalised roses. The castle is interesting in merging the Polesworth dockyard style of towers and roofs, learnt while an apprentice, with windows and details in a Braunston style, where he did most of his painting.*

from the heart. One or two painters use the symmetrical pattern of two paired main petals with small strokes round the border, suggesting the dog rose rather than the cultivated one, while the Stoke-on-Trent painter uses the strokes very subtly to suggest the edges of the petals, achieving a great deal more realism than is usual. Otherwise, it must be admitted, although pretty and floral in concept, the decorations have little in common with roses. Their attractiveness is as much due to the abstract pattern of brush strokes as it is to their botany. The simpler roses are then completed with dashes of deep colour in the centres, streaks of white to highlight the red petals and sometimes a little group of yellow stamens to each. The group is then finished off by painting the veins of the leaves in yellow or pale green.

Fig. 24 *The basic petal pattern of seven different painters.*

The painting of castle panels cannot be broken down quite so easily to a set of basic essentials, although there are certain ingredients common to so many styles that they can be considered part of a traditional design. All have a mountainous background landscape and make much use of water, the sea or a lake in the distance and a river, or possibly canal, in the foreground. All have sailing boats and trees, and most have a bridge. Sunsets and swans would seem to be a northern prerogative however, while massive castellations and clustered groups of flat-topped towers are found further south. Further generalisations would be misleading because of the number of exceptions.

The method of painting is fairly straightforward and logical; the sky is painted first right across the allotted space, strong blue at the top paling almost to white at the horizon. The same brushes can be used to paint an area of water right across the bottom half at the same time. White clouds are painted into the wet sky with one or two direct strokes, and the mountains put into the background with a few sweeps of the blue brush. After dragging some reflection into the water area with the same brush it must be left a while to dry, or the following stages become unmanageable. This is no great drawback to the dock painter working on a complete cabin, or a series of objects, as he will move on and paint the skies for all the castle panels, then perhaps the leaves for the roses. By the time he has completed that section the sky is sufficiently dry to proceed to the next stage, and so on, with never a moment wasted. Only by this method is he able to decorate the inside of the cabin completely in one day, which in the heyday of the canal was the usual time allowed.

The next step is the castle building itself, painted as a series of cylinders and boxes, yellowy cream on the sunny side shaded to umber in the shadows. No details are put in yet, until the ground and any masses of trees have been blocked in and everything allowed to dry off again. Then the painter works into it with a small sable-haired brush, neatening up the edges, and drawing in the details of windows, doors, bridges and stonework with black or dark brown. Sailing boats, trees, bushes and flagpoles

37 *Castle by an unidentified painter on one of two doors that were presented by the Severn & Canal Carrying Co to Birmingham museum in 1937; paradoxically, they did not have any decoration on their boats. Reproduced by permission of the Birmingham Museum and Art Gallery.*

are put in at this stage, leaving only the finishing touches to complete the work, for example white sails and highlights, bright red roofs and flags, and the main colours of trees and ornamental bushes.

A final characteristic shared by the majority is the friendly atmosphere which seems to pervade the painting. It is rather like a large country house compared with a castle, with a pleasant air of security. Do they symbolise the boatman's feeling of security in his waterborne home, or his longing for security in a house on the bank? Perhaps a little of both.

The paints used today are quick-drying oil paints in tubes made specially for signwriters, but this is a recent development. Artists' oil colours have been available in tubes since the last century, but they are expensive and slow drying. Some canal painters used them, but the majority bought their pigment in powder form and mixed up small batches for themselves with linseed oil as and when they needed it. Before World War II much of the ordinary paint of the dock was bought in paste form, the pigment ground into linseed oil and sold in 1cwt drums; small amounts were used by the fancy-painter. Even then the best bright red, vermilion, was still bought as powder in small leather bags and because of its cost was used with moderation and care. In both cases, a little terebine or paste drier was added to shorten drying time, and turpentine used to thin it to a workable consistency. Goldsize added to the oil also speeded drying and gave a matt finish to provide a better key for the final essential varnishing. The dry pigments could also be mixed with a water-based medium if desired, for example gum or gluesize, just strong enough to hold the paint in place until the overall varnish bound it more firmly together to protect it from wear. This meant that the whole process of painting and varnishing could be done in one day, but it does not seem to have been common, and was unlikely to have been so hard wearing as oil-based paint.

Although many boatmen have achieved wonders with dreadful old paint brushes, the professionals save much time and aggravation by using the very best sable hair signwriting brushes. Even the best of craftsmen have difficulty doing good work with inferior tools, especially when much of the charm of the work is in the smooth pattern of confident brush strokes as in canal flowers. A small wooden palette is useful to mix small amounts of colour, but old tobacco tins, large enough for the quantities of semi-runny paint needed to work all round the boat, are probably more usual. The final piece of equipment usual to the boat painter is the mahl stick, a cane with a padded end to rest against the boat; it is held in the left hand, and provides a steady support for the right hand while signwriting. It is very useful when working over or into wet paint.

In turning now to the work of individual narrow boat artists I must stress that I have not attempted to provide a complete list but have analysed and described the work of a few painters of the last 50 years, helped by recollections of people who knew them, who could be said to be typical characters following the

38 *Tom Ditton using mahl stick and palette whilst signwriting the wartime utility initials on a butty at the Grand Union Canal Carrying Company's dock at Bulls Bridge in 1944.*

calling of the professional dockyard painter.

Perhaps the most important recent painter on the northern canals was William Hodgson, the painter for the Anderton Company in Stoke-on-Trent. This company had always been one of the larger canal carriers in the North West, originally based at Anderton, but moving to a new dock in Middleport in the 1880s. The dock maintained a large fleet, and gained many of the customers of both William's dock in Middlewich, and Fox's dock at Longport as each closed during the 1930s. Its life was again boosted when the Mersey-Weaver Carrying Company took over the whole firm just after World War II, and closed its own dock down, continuing to use the old Anderton Company dock. Thus the dock and the painter are both very important to the later history of canal painting, for they were kept busy until 1958, maintaining a live and healthy tradition.

As it was one of the larger canal dockyards, even employing two or three straight painters in addition to the boatbuilders, there was enough work to keep Bill Hodgson employed solely as decorator and signwriter, in contrast to most of the dock painters who were primarily boat builders, with painting as a second string. This constant practice must have added considerably to his natural skill. He was known to have had theatrical scenery painting experience when young, and some training at the Northwich School of Art. He also seems to have been a compulsive painter – his work was not confined to working hours at the dock, but spread to his house and furniture too. He worked at William's dock in Middlewich for a time but was working at Samuel Fox's dock at Westport Lake when it closed about 1935. He transferred to the Middleport dock when the Anderton Company took over, and worked alongside their resident signwriter and decorator Charlie Adams who died a couple of years later. Hodgson remained there until ill health forced him to retire a few years before the dock closed, when Harold Hood the dock-foreman took over the decorative painting in Hodgson's style, although Bill still did a considerable amount of work at home. He died in 1959.

There seems to be a theatrical quality to his castle scenes, where he uses a sunset as a regular feature, with a dramatically outlined mountain background. Castles are always symmetrical, usually of three squat towers with three heavy castellations to each of the outside ones. As the space to be filled grows higher in proportion to its breadth, so the castle grows another set of smaller towers behind, the central one often with a pointed spire complete with cross. The building is set centrally on a hill, with a lake behind it stretching back to the mountains, with white-sailed boats in the middle distance on each side. The foreground may be another stretch of water, sometimes with a couple of swans floating gracefully in the reflection of the castle hill. The list of Hodgson main ingredients is completed with a path or drive leading up to the one central doorway, coming in from the right of the picture on the larger panels, or straight up, vanishing strongly in perspective on narrow panels where the foreground water is excluded.

In common with many other dockyards, all paintwork on the outside of the boat was put on the owner's bill, while any decoration

39 *A handbowl painted by William Hodgson. The way that the Player's cigarette sailor's head trademark caught the boatman's fancy and was accepted as part of his own tradition of painting restates the possibility that the roses and castles were also adopted from another field at an earlier date.*

painted inside the boatman's cabin, other than the plain oak graining and perhaps one or two castles, was paid for separately by the captain. This led in many cases to a much more imaginative treatment inside the cabins according to the captain's taste. On this work Bill showed much originality. Castle scenes developed into more general landscapes with groups of cottages clustered around a church, or a Tudor-style farmhouse complete with ducks and cows. The Player's packet sailor's head and crinoline ladies were used quite often on the table-cupboard panel, and being a good animal painter, Bill Hodgson used pictures of dogs and horses regularly. Possibly the best example of his work was a large painting, on the wall above the side bed, of four or five racehorses galloping past the finishing post. His flowers are undoubtedly the finest from the point of view of realism. They have depth, and it is obvious that he made a real study of the rose shape and form as his technique developed. Inside the cabin they were often arranged as a picture, an oval shape painted on the wall, complete with frame, string and nail from which to hang it! As one boat-woman put it, 'you didn't need no hanging plates and lace in one of his cabins'.

His style is important for it forms the root of much of the work by northern boatman painters. As the flowers need more time and care spent on them than the simpler southern pattern there are correspondingly fewer boatman painters who work in this style. They have formalised Bill's artistic approach a little to reduce it to a more memorable method. Perhaps because his usual castle is so symmetrical, and is thus easier to systemise and remember, it is rather more popular. Certainly the three towers, with three castellations, on a central hill, turn up in work that is otherwise dissimilar.

J. Harry Taylor, of Chester, is another interesting painter of the northern narrow canals. He died in 1924 so my comments on his boat painting must be based on photographic evidence, although several of his paintings exist, owned by his family and friends, though they were produced primarily as pictures rather than as applied decoration. He developed an interest in boat painting and painting in general from a friend who was a theatrical scene-painter. It is repeated as family history that he upset the dock-painter at his father's boatbuilding yard in Walsall by experimenting with his paints and brushes after business hours, an understandable craftsman's reaction. He inherited the business in 1889 at the age of 23, but moved to Gobowen in 1909, and to premises at Chester in 1911. He finally set up in 1916 in the Dee basin, the lowest intermediate pound of the three locks dropping into the river Dee, where many Mersey flats and barges were docked as well as narrow boats.

When the Shropshire Union Company gave up carrying in 1921 and sold its fleet, some customers took up the transport of their own goods in ex-SUC boats. Taylors took over the boatbuilding yard, and acquired more narrow boat business with the new concerns, so we can assume that there was more decorative painting to be done.

From photographs it is obvious that he was a very good signwriter making considerable use of decorative lettering on cabin sides compared to the more usual Ionic or Egyptian lettering discussed previously. His castles appear very medieval and solid and firmly within the conventions, although his flowers do not seem to fit into any canal style.

His paintings on canvas are the work of an accomplished amateur, quite presentable although full of mannerisms and techniques, but far better than most straightforward dock painters could manage. They are painstaking and it is obvious that his method of painting on boats must have been much more commercialised for, in common with other dock painters, he could work through all the decorative painting on a boat in a couple of days, a speed which demands a very professional approach. As an amateur artist, however, his extra skill could explain some of the oddities that crop up in the narrow boat tradition. Like Bill Hodgson he was capable of painting almost anything if asked, and the 'Stag at Bay' that appears on the cabin block in a photograph of a Shropshire Union boat would present more of a challenge than a problem to him.

After J. Harry Taylor died, the castles and lettering were done

40 *The signwriting and decorative work of J. Harry Taylor, photographed in the Chester dry dock in the early twenties.*

by his son Wilf Taylor. Although satisfactory, he was not quite as proficient as his father, and rather than paint his castles freehand he used to copy a picture of the King Charles Tower in Chester on to the boats; this became a sort of trademark of Taylor's docking. The Ceriog Granite Company's boats off the Llangollen Canal also used a real place on their boats, Chirk Castle, but apart from these two examples real castles do not seem to have been common.

The yard at Polesworth on the Coventry Canal, belonging to Messrs Lees & Atkins, has an important place in this chapter, as it had a very good reputation, particularly among the owner-boatmen of the Oxford and Grand Union Canals, for turning out a sound and splendid looking job. The number ones, as noted earlier, were almost fanatical about their boats' appearance and rivalry was intense; the bounds of the decorative tradition were reached and pushed outwards by this yard. Each succeeding boat must better the last man's and have one or two unique features. They developed the use of the Union Flag as a decorative device on the cratch, and painted flowers in every available place; borders around the name panels on cabin sides multiplied, and complicated designs of diamonds extended all over the boat, equipment and horse harness. The bobbins, feed tin and spreader were left with the boat for painting during docking, while the boatman could hire one of Lee & Atkins' own fully equipped 'change' boats which were kept solely for their customers' use while their own craft were on the slipway. A mutual trust operated between this class of customer and Polesworth dock, with many boats being built and repaired on a hire purchase arrangement, the boatman paying a little each time he came by, or so much per trip. With much of their pre-war business based on this group, they were badly hit by the closure of some of the local canalside coalmines combined with the takeover of many of the small coal hauliers by companies acting as agents for the majority of their traffic anyway. These companies were the Samuel Barlow Coal Company and S. E. Barlow's, two separate firms carrying similar cargoes but each with their own docks or arrangements with other yards, and therefore with no need to patronise Polesworth dock. Lees &

41 *William Smith's boats provide a fine example of the high competitive standards maintained amongst the Grand Junction owner boatmen.*

Atkins laid off men and closed down in 1938, although the firm continued in a much smaller way of business into the 1950s under the brothers Jim and Isaiah Atkins.

The company had been in existence since the 1900s and was run in the 1920s by Harry Atkins (Mr Lees had been a butcher and a sleeping partner only) and it was he who did all the signwriting work as well as boat building, while his sons Jim and Isaiah handled the other decorative paintwork, both in a similar style. It is an easily recognisable pattern when it has once become familiar. The rose flowers are broad, made up of four main petal strokes, two smaller ones at the base, with as many as six or seven tiny strokes forming the leading edge, or heart of the flower. They are always firmly based on the same pattern with tiny strokes thin enough to be thick stamens, suggesting the wild dogrose more than the cultivated flower. They are obviously painted fast and confidently with petal colours brushed on before the underpainting has dried, giving a subtle gradation of colour at the middle of the flower and differing from the hard edged neatness of other painters.

42 *One of the castles painted in the boathouse of Snarestone Lodge on the Ashby canal by Isaiah Atkins of Lees & Atkins dock at Polesworth. The spray patterns of windows, round tower roofs, waterside rushes and large bridge are all typical Polesworth ingredients.*

The castles are a central group of three or four round towers and adjoining square buildings with red pitched roofs. The towers are an instantly recognisable characteristic, always painted with many long church windows arranged in a spray pattern with little serious attempt at realism, surmounted by roofs that may best be described as fancy red or blue saucepan lids. There is always a pond in foreground with bunches of coloured rushes along the side; the water sometimes runs back under an oversize bridge leading out of the first floor level with the whole castle unit very often leaning to the left. They are painted with great confidence, the details drawn in with a soft transparent umber and are castles of charming *naïveté*, masterpieces of folk art.

The only survivor of the several docks formerly on the Oxford Canal is at Banbury. It is run by Herbert Tooley, whose family have owned it since 1900, and who must be one of the last all-round canal craftsmen, capable of doing all the work involved in boat docking from caulking to painting castles. He learnt the trade from his father George Tooley, whose painting is described so well in L. T. C. Rolt's *Narrow Boat*. The relevant passage is quoted in Appendix 5. The Tooley roses have similarities with the symmetrical Polesworth flowers and it would be interesting to know whether the same master craftsman trained apprentices Tooley and Atkins.

The painted work from the dockyard at Braunston has had a strong influence on the narrow boat tradition for at least the last 50 years. It is ideally placed to develop that influence, at the cross roads of the Coventry and Oxford canal route with the Birmingham to London line of the Grand Union Canal. Much of the southward traffic on both routes during these 50 years consisted of coal, and most of Nurser Bros boatyard's trade was on coal boats, paradoxically the most highly decorated.

The family business was started in 1878 by William Nurser, but by 1928 two of his sons, Charles and Frank, were trading as Nurser Bros, Charles concentrating on the boat building side while Frank managed the office work and much of the painting.

43 *Frank Nurser at work at Braunston in 1948.*

Although Nurser Bros was a boat building firm, building for companies all over the canal system, the majority of the work comprised regular repairs and maintenance, where the painter's trade was of greater importance than usual. The firm was certainly well known for the standard of its paintwork during the 1930s, an unusually high reputation for a small dockyard employing only six or seven men. Both Frank and Charles were good painters, and one of their apprentices, Percy Foster, was generally regarded as being as good as his master (although not by Frank Nurser himself) painting pictures in addition to his canal work. Any boatbuilder worth his keep was expected to handle a paintbrush respectably at Nurser's yard. It catered for some of the Grand Junction 'number ones' with their competitive demands for more decoration, and had a long-standing arrangement for the building and maintenance of the Samuel Barlow Coal Company fleet. This company, after taking over many of the boats of the independent boatmen, completed its expansion by buying out Braunston dockyard in 1941.

As Charles retired from the firm when it was taken over, and Percy Foster unfortunately died shortly afterwards, there was too much decorative work for one man to handle, particularly as Frank had agreed to carry on as manager as well. A considerable amount of the decoration then fell to the new dock foreman George Crowshaw who had transferred from the other Barlow boat dock at Tamworth. With the work of the Nursers and their apprentice constantly before him, it is not surprising that his painting has a clear Braunston stamp to it, although he served his boat building apprenticeship at Lees & Atkins' yard. Although not as fluent and graceful as Frank Nurser's work, Crowshaw's painting is very satisfactory.

Another boatbuilder whose style of painting shows a strong Braunston influence is Jess Owen, now working and painting at Charity Dock, Bedworth. Although apprenticed at the Mersey-Weaver Company dock in the Potteries, he did no canal painting at all until he worked at Barlow's dock at Braunston after World War II, and only very little then until he moved to Bedworth where

44 *The cabin doors of the* Hardy *in 1961, the decorative work of George Crowshaw.*

there was nobody else to do it. The fact that Nurser worked in the office and thus did less heavy work than the majority of professional dock painters, may partly account for the good quality of his work, appearing as it does more the work of an artist than a decorative formula.

In the late 1940s two of the lads working at the yard, Ron Hough and Dennis Clark, both showed an interest and some talent in boat painting and Frank Nurser started to teach them the trade. After a serious illness it is Ron Hough's opinion that Nurser's teaching became even more precise, as if to ensure the trade's continuation should anything happen to him. Alas, it did, and Frank Nurser

45 *A large cabin block decorated by Frank Nurser in the 1940's. Although characteristic, it is by a man who had been painting for forty years, and has lost some of the subtlety of his earlier work.*

died in 1952 but left his style and standards imprinted on the long-lived and well decorated boats of the Barlow fleet and their successors, a legacy that could be the logical continuation of a line of painters stretching back to the early days of the canals.

Nurser's style of flower painting is a little difficult to describe, for, although recognisable by its skill, the actual pattern of brush-strokes varies considerably. They usually start on one larger petal stroke with a series of smaller strokes to complement it. The hearts of the roses are dark, the colour worked into the undercoat disc while still wet, and are finished with three or four little yellow stamens. Leaves follow no formal arrangement of size or design but always seem to complete the group naturally. Daisy-like flowers appear everywhere in all sorts of colour combinations. The space in the centre of a group of roses is sometimes painted with an overall background colour, and the whole area painted with a mass of tiny blooms, a very distinctive Nurser design now sometimes seen in the work of Ron Hough. His castles are much more believable than the majority of canal pictures although still often including such features as a round tower with one huge battlement slot. Characteristic is the gable end of a building, the peak of which rises above the roof to form a chimney-like structure, a feature that appears regularly in all the Braunston style painters' work. Compositions generally feature a cluster of straight round towers with dark cappings, several red pitched roofs with fancy ridged tiles and white highlights, an orange forecourt, and much use of ornamental bushes and trees. Details are drawn in quite heavily with a dark brown giving a rich warmth to the finished picture. Like Bill Hodgson, Nurser was not limited to castles alone; he painted landscapes, horses' heads, dogs' heads (generally a St Bernard) and sometimes used a single swan as a subject. Flowers were sometimes painted as a bunch complete with the stems in a vase or as a single bud on a sprig of leaves. It is difficult to judge why these unusual designs were not more common. Certainly the decorative skills were present, if dormant, in many boatyards for a more adventurous treatment.

46 *The confidence of every brushstroke is apparent in this typical castle by Frank Nurser.*

Fellows, Morton & Clayton have been mentioned several times, for, apart from being one of the largest independent carriers, it set high standards of maintenance and of crews. It owned two boatyards to service its fleet, although much of the new boat building was contracted out to other yards. One yard was at Saltley in Birmingham and concentrated on maintenance of boats working in the North West area, while the other at Uxbridge looked after the Boats on the Grand Union route. Although the firm was renowned for its businesslike efficiency and cost consciousness it never tried to economise by reducing the amount of decoration. It was an accepted principle that apart from being good for the worker/management relationship, a boatman protecting his beautiful paintwork was also protecting the company's boat.

The decorative painter at Saltley just before World War II was George Preston. He appears in a group photograph of the dock staff of 1894, and might have served his apprenticeship there. It is possible that he was in a self-employed capacity by the 1930s as on FM&C's recommendation he became the decorator for Yarwood's shipyard in Northwich as well. He was originally sent there to decorate some of FM&C's own new boats and was

47 *The painting of George Preston photographed at Yarwoods dockyard at Northwich during the thirties.*

afterwards regularly called in to paint boats built there for other companies, for example those of Associated Canal Carriers and Cowburn & Cowpar. He went to Northwich by train from Birmingham and would complete the decoration in one day, returning home in the evening. This was presumably just the roses and castles as, apart from the impossibility of doing the lettering as well in just one day, Yarwood's employed their own excellent signwriter, David Dykes.

At the Uxbridge yard the decorative painting work was shared by Henry Penn who graduated to foreman-painter from a blacksmith's striker, and Harry Crook a boatbuilder. Signwriting was done by an outside signwriter, Mr Osborne, who could write a motor boat's cabin sides complete with blocking out and two coats of paint on the letters in one day, a speed unlikely to be achieved by a part-timer. The Uxbridge flowers have neither the flamboyance nor the nonchalance of the Braunston work; their charm relies more on their neatness and the formality of the groups. All the flowers are based on a similar pattern, a nearly circular crescent surrounded by a pattern of small fat petals, backed by a tidy design of equal sized leaves. It may be that it is a development of George Preston's style, whose flowers are similarly constructed, or possibly of a previous FM&C style common to all of them. Because of its relative simplicity, and its widespread use in this important firm it is a flower pattern that often turns up in the boatman painter's work.

When the young Grand Union Canal Carrying Company was expanding courageously in the early 1930s, the modern image that it was trying to foster did not include the traditional roses and castles. Although the company altered its original colour scheme of two shades of blue to a more traditional red, white and blue in 1937, it still excluded any curving designs or unnecessary frills. The company seems to have softened its attitude as time went by, perhaps because it had constant difficulty in finding enough crews. There was considerable opposition to the wartime utility painting scheme which again tried to simplify paintwork. By nationalisation in 1948 the curving shape on the back of the doors had returned

48 *A pair of British waterways boats at the Inland Waterways Association rally of boats at Market Harborough in 1950. The extra line bordering the name panel and the* fleur de lys *in the corners were soon regarded as unnecessary frills and deleted. The castle on the canvas flap is by Tom Ditton, probably commissioned by the boatman himself.*

and roses and castles had re-appeared, though perhaps unofficially, on water cans and cabin doors. Some were painted by the boatmen themselves but others were by the painter/signwriter at the new depot at Bulls Bridge, Tom Ditton. He had transferred from nearby Hizzard's dock which the new yard had superseded in 1936, and he stayed until he retired in 1957. In an initial burst of enthusiasm the new British Waterways management started having the boats properly decorated again by Tom Ditton, but a further directive soon cut back all 'unnecessary' expense. This caused a considerable public row as it was seen as bureaucratic interference with a traditional way of life, particularly as the previously decorated fleet of Fellows, Morton & Clayton was also now affected. The resulting compromise was the introduction of transfers. Although designed by another of the most traditional of canal painters, Frank Jones of Leighton Buzzard, they lacked the individuality and spontaneity of the real thing, and became boringly common. They remained in use until the fleet ceased carrying. It was a sad and too nearly successful move to abandon a symbol of the boat people's trade identity.

49 *The standard British Waterways transfers in use on the motor boat* Tarporley *in 1963. If it were not for the boatman's own decorative additions it would be difficult to believe that narrow boats were ever renowned for an abundance of designs and patterns.*

CHAPTER 5

BCN Boats and their Paintwork

The network of canals in and around Birmingham and the Black Country bred a rather different style of boat decoration because of the short-haul system of boats and boating. While the Trent & Mersey or the Oxford and Grand Junction Canals were important as through routes, particularly connections between import/export docks and industrial centres inland, a major proportion of the Birmingham area's huge traffic was short-haul coal. Initially coal was mined near Birmingham and dispatched outwards. Then, as local pits were worked out and the heavy engineering side of Birmingham industry was expanding, inwards coal from Cannock Chase pits became an increasingly important part of the trade. The original Birmingham Canal Company had amalgamated with the Birmingham & Fazely Company and soon afterwards, in 1794, changed its name to the Birmingham Canal Navigations (BCN). It was a forward-looking group, and joined forces with the Wyrley & Essington and Dudley Canal companies when the railway threat emerged to form strong opposition. Although it came under railway domination, its efficiency ensured its survival, and the BCN ran as an economic unit well into the twentieth century. The policy of the controlling railway interest was to encourage short distance traffic to and from the crowded metropolis, where new railway sidings were already impracticable, and to use the canals to feed their railway depots with long distance work, an internally successful policy, although giving little benefit to the rest of the canal system.

A contributing factor to this success was the day-boat system. When the longest regular runs in the coal trade were no more than 25 or 30 miles, there was no necessity for a fully developed

50 *A confusion of BCN coal boats waiting to load at Hednesford basin on the Cannock extension.*

living cabin, as the boatman could complete his journey and return home nightly, or at least every alternate day. The boats could also be used as floating storage; the boatman delivered a loaded boat and changed directly into an empty boat for the return journey. The craft that developed from this method of working were called day-boats or joey-boats, as opposed to the long distance cabin-boats. Severely utilitarian, with a very straight stem and stern, they were built to take the maximum possible load and are relatively unattractive to look at, although they 'swam' surprisingly well at horse speed, considering their simplicity. Some had no cabin at all, but the majority had a small box cabin aft, sufficient to house a small, coalfired bottle stove for brewing up hot drinks and a fixed cross-bed for an overnight stay if necessary. Most boats were double-enders, with provision in the stem and stern posts for the helm to be hung at either end; this removed the difficulty on an ordinary cabin-boat of travelling stern first out of restricted canal arms to the nearest winding hole or junction to turn the boat. Normally they were worked with the cabin astern for the comfort of the boat steerer.

With this different method of work, there was not the same feeling of pride amongst the boatmen in the individual boat and consequently less individual care and decoration. Roses and castles were unknown in the day-boats and only appeared latterly on some of the tugs of the coal hauliers, where the same captain used the same boat every day and occasionally lived aboard. There were, however, other conventions of decorative painting on these boats, although with more of a trade mark quality compared to the family cabin boats. The standard would seem to have been set for the esteem of the company rather than the pride of the boatman.

As the joeys were open boats with no foredeck, and had no top cloths with their associated equipment of mast, stands, and planks, all decoration was confined to the top bends or planks at the bow and stern, known respectively as the 'fore end' and 'shoulders', and the little box cabin with its slide and doors. To even the score a little, more varied use was made of the fore end sections than on the long distance boats with their usually bold and simple designs. In comparison they presented a very symbolical appearance, with varicoloured circles, crescents and diamonds, often quartered into four separate colours on, usually, a bright red background. More

51 *One of the first motor tugs to work the BCN pictured outside Walker's yard, Rickmansworth, where she was built in 1919. The roses and castles put on the doors may have set a fashion for future tugs to follow.*

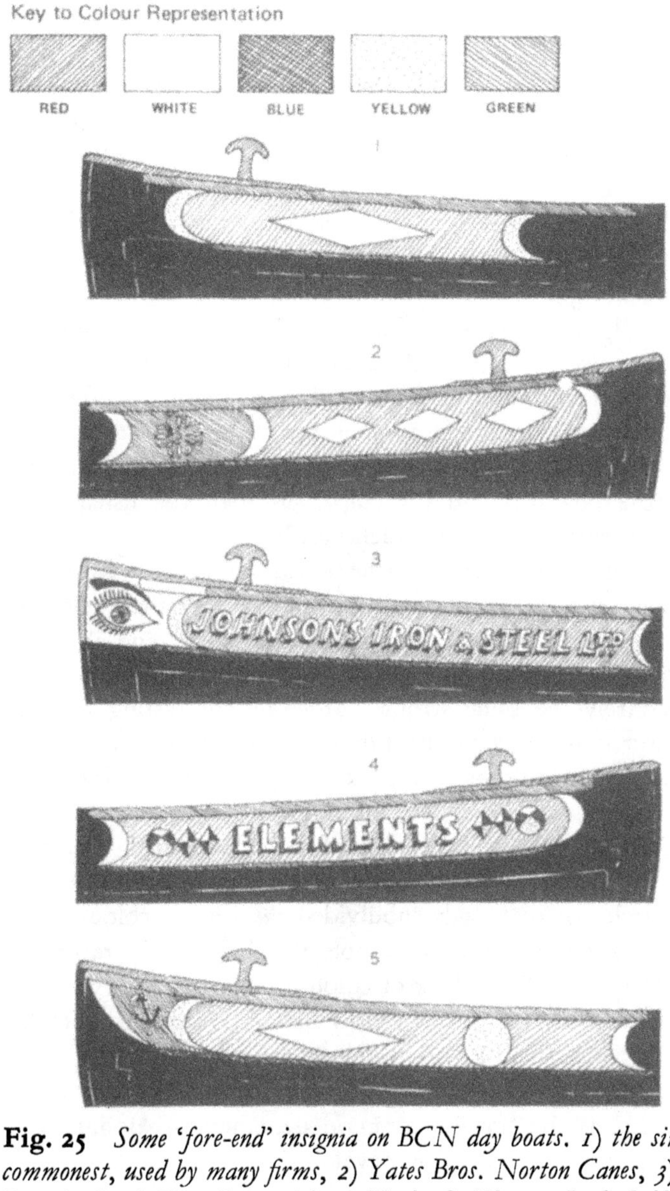
Key to Colour Representation
RED
WHITE
BLUE
YELLOW
GREEN
1
2
3
JOHNSONS IRON & STEEL LTD
4
ELEMENTS
5

Fig. 25 *Some 'fore-end' insignia on BCN day boats. 1) the simplest and commonest, used by many firms, 2) Yates Bros. Norton Canes, 3) Johnson's Iron & Steel, West Bromwich, 4) T. & S. Element Ltd, Salford Bridge, 5) Arthur Cooper, Rolt Street, Birmingham.*

use was made of individual firms' trademarks and trade symbols, as well as the occasional pun (like a painted section of brick wall on the fore ends of Wall's boats) and the whole effect was often of coded messages. In one sense at least they were. Because of the day boat system and the great numbers of boats waiting about empty or loaded, it was important to recognise one firm's boats from another with some speed and certainty, and various design combinations were of more use to an illiterate boatman than any amount of writing. Most of the Birmingham area boats had painted names as well, although some firms merely gave them numbers. Each boat was also allotted an official number when new and gauged for the first time. Later, by measuring average draught and referring to the table under its number, the weight carried could be calculated and tolls charged accordingly. Boats were given names more for the boatman and his employer, than the usual canal bye-law requirement of positive identification.

By far the most usual colour scheme throughout the BCN was bright red and green. Less effort was taken to ensure that they were separated by a light colour than on the cabin-boats, and although there was often a cream dividing line between areas of colour, there was rarely the same strong border of contrasting tone so characteristic of long distance boat decoration. This was particularly noticeable on the fore ends where the whole available width of the top plank was usually red, less often green, and the symbol or writing was placed along the middle of the colour block. Compare this with the treatment of the general carrying boats, where any symbols, circles or diamonds subdivided the central colour shape between the usual border which echoes the shape of the top plank from top to bottom. The block of colour on the fore end was then finished off at each end with a yellow or white crescent, with the convex side to the front. This panel, starting on the plank a few inches clear of the stempost and ending just before the boat achieved its full width, is the 'lowest common denominator' design from which individual firms' insignia develop. The fore end is reserved for the firm's name or design, sometimes a combination of the two as on the coal boats belonging to T & S Elements, where the

signwriting was always bracketed by the firms standard pattern
code of two diamonds and a circle, quartered into four colours.
The shoulders carried the boat's own name or number, put on a
similar panel to the fore end, but with the crescents bending towards
the stern post. Again this was the simplest basic ground. In both
cases the top of the wooden guard below the panel was painted
green or blue to contrast with the red, and the thin iron 'fancy'
guard protecting the top edge of the plank was similarly treated.
More scope was achieved by painting right forward on to the sides
of stempost or by subdividing the panel again with further
crescents or circles, and alternating the ground colour. Diamonds
were rarely used in the familiar cabin-boat way, as an area decorated
by an overall diagonal design, but were used as separate symbols.
Several firms used one white diamond painted on the red ground
as part of their insignia (Mitchards, Stewarts & Lloyds and the
Wulfruna Coal Company are examples) but three white diamonds
in line was the trademark of the Yates Brothers fleet from Norton
Canes only. Easier to interpret was the symbol of Pearson's bottle
works, a white silhouette of a bottle on a red ground, with the
name *Pearson* written on the bottle. Most extraordinary were the
craft belonging to Johnson's Iron & Steel Company which had a
large and powerful eye painted on each side at the top of the

52 *A boat docked and painted at Peter Keay and Son's dock at Walsall;
signwriting by Ken Keay.*

stempost as well as the complete Company name on the fore end panels; it is presumably an initial 'eye' for Iron, but gives a splendid impetus to the 'oculus' tradition mentioned before.

The name or number was painted on the shoulders at the stern with a strong two-tone shadow adding richness to the simplest block letters. On a red background the shadow was usually green or blue and black behind a white or cream letter. Even when the boat had only a number, it was written on with style; the 'N' of 'No' had long freehand serif flourishes, and the italic numerals a strong contrast between thick and thin strokes.

The joey-boat rudder shows a sharp contrast to the elegantly painted ram's head of the family boat. It was built a little lighter for ease in changing from one boat to another, with the lower pintle or 'bottom hanging' pivoting on one bolt, so that it would fit various sizes of boats. The paintwork is severe, with only the stock, 'top tingles' or floats, and bracket in different colours, with no attempt at the fancy bordering or disguising patterns noted earlier. Even the circle over the top of the stock was missing, but it must be borne in mind that the rudder served a rough life, being banged from boat to boat daily, with consequent wear and tear. The tiller, though, being lighter and handled more gently, followed the common practice of being striped in four or five sections across its length.

Like the rudder, the towing mast lacked decoration for it was the size and shape of a young telegraph pole on a day-boat, and the consequent awkwardness in changing boats would soon remove any paint.

After World War II, seldom was much time or effort put into painting cabin sides as before, nor was as much trouble ever taken over them as on the long distance boats. Some cabins were simply gas-tarred black all over, which would seem to be the most practical scheme on a coal boat; others had a small panel or name-plate painted near the back of the cabin, while the rest were painted in the full colours, usually red and green, although sometimes only lettered with the initials of the steerage company. Lawrence Miller's Birmingham horse boats were in a slate grey and white

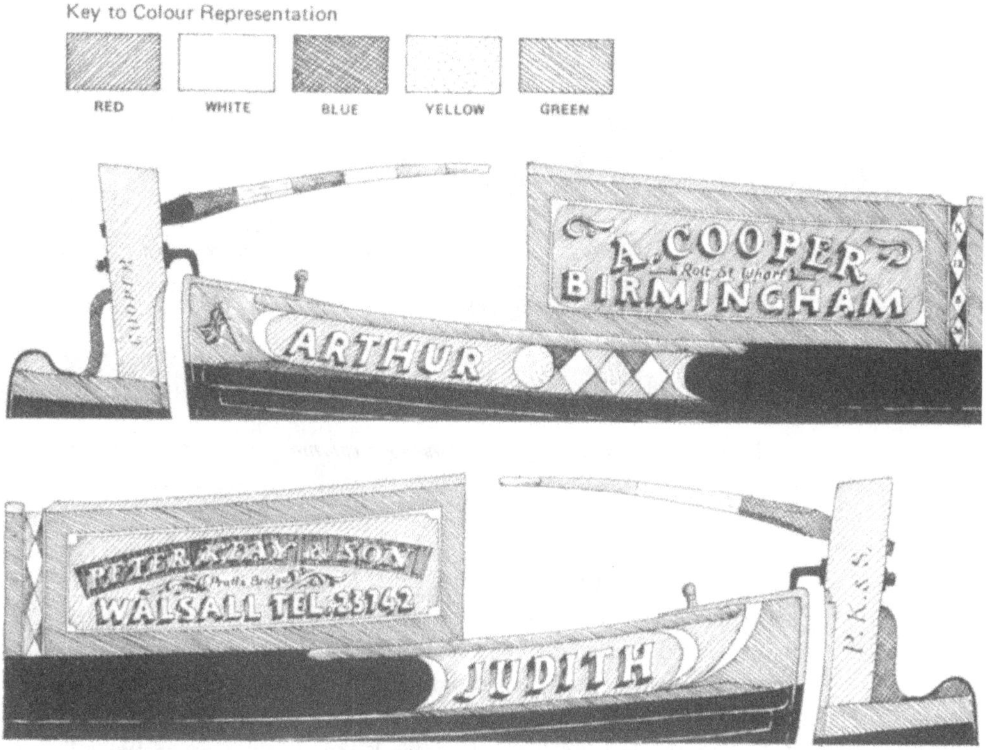

Fig. 26 *Two of the most decorative company colour schemes of the BCN. Few firms went to this much trouble since the introduction of motor tugs.*

colour scheme. Nevertheless the generalisation remains true – a red or green nameplate with a four or five inch border of strong green or red to contrast, separated by a very thin line of white or yellow. This $\frac{1}{4}$ in line was thickened at the corners to give a rounded outline to the main panel, which with plain boarding did not have to conform to any structural design here, as it did on the cabin boats with their added panelling and moulding. Some boats were on almost permanent hire from large firms of boatbuilders; cabin sides were thus divided in two, with one half bearing the owner's name and address, and the other that of the hirer. In some cases the hirer used the whole of the cabin side, and the actual ownership

53 *A coal boat on dock in 1931, showing a common cabin side layout and the trademark pattern on the back of the cabin as used by Peter Keay & Son's dock. Lettering is by Peter Keay.*

was only apparent from the design on the shoulders.

Sometimes a band of diamonds appeared in a line below the gap at the end of the cabin cant or handrail, where the rainwater drained from the roof. Each diamond, in the normal narrow boat colour sequence, bears a number or letter, describing the place and date of the last docking. If Peter Keay's dockyard of Walsall, which used this form of advertisement, finished work on a boat on 10 May 1958, the top diamond had a 'K' in it, the next the figure 10, next the month 5, and the bottom diamond bore 58; other dockyards had their own specific marks, 'W Ltd.' for Worsey's dock and 'Y' for Yates Brothers for example.

Another design which owed much to the dockyard where it was painted, was the shape that appears on the outside of the doors of the cabin. In its simplest form – the one that appears country-wide on narrow boats – it simply rises to a point in the middle and curves out and down to the top of the hatches, and is known as the 'saddle'. Several Black Country docks, however, developed their own extreme variations which, in the absence of a customer's specification, they would put on any boat docked and painted by them, and which was regarded as a trademark.

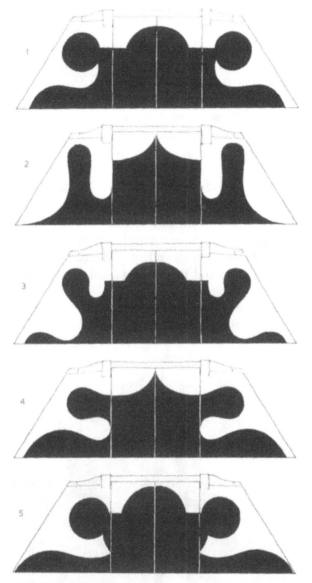

Fig. 27 *Black Country dockyard variations of the design on the back of the cabin. 1) Worsey's Ltd, Walsall, 2) Yates Bros, Norton Canes, 3) Peter Keay & Son, Walsall, 4) seen on a boat belonging to E. W. Reed, 5) a Worsey variation for Leonard Leigh's boats.*

When the horse boat was king on the BCN, most cabins were signwritten in full with the name of the owner and his business address, with perhaps some scrolls to finish the effect. With the advent of motorboats, however, to pull trains of boats around, expensive signwriting costs were saved for the tugs. Such names as *Hector*, *Primus*, *Typhoon*, and *Tornado* give us an idea of the pride with which they were first regarded, and as the tugs were no doubt worked hard and regularly to pay for themselves, cabin sides were given the full treatment. They would have the complete name and address of the company with a descriptive phrase like 'canal haulage' or 'boat steerage' and telephone number painted in script between. The names of firm and boat were in large, proud letters with heavy serifs (known sensibly as 'tailed letters') and the town's name in large block letters. All characters were deeply shadowed or blocked and the corners filled with a baroque scroll

54 *This Black Country tug shows an interesting mixture of long distance narrow boat conventions, the water can, ram's head and roses on cabin side and pigeon box, with the coal boat door panels and the powerful lettering and scrolls typical of the motor tug.*

to enhance the majesty of the motor's power. Again like the horse boats, the most usual colour scheme was red and green with a yellow line between, but there were exceptions. The Leonard Leigh fleet of tugs and boats, was painted in black, white and grey livery although this was a relatively recent innovation to contrast with the more usual red and green.

The notable thing about the decoration of the Birmingham area was its very vigorous independence as a tradition. It was not just a remnant of the long distance boat's treatment, but had a separate existence altogether. Many of the ingredients obviously stemmed from the same root, but whether the BCN style of paintwork was nearer the original pattern than the rose and castle technique will probably remain an interesting mystery. This independence was highlighted by the Samuel Barlow Coal Company, which had a fleet of long distance boats renowned for the high standard of decoration on the Grand Union Canal, and a fleet of Birmingham coal boats working from a separate dockyard. At times they worked over the same routes. Here one would expect a fusion of the two styles but the coal boats remained simple, with a green nameplate, broad yellow border and just the initials on the cabin side, with no decorative device at all on the fore end, while the cabin boats continued to carry the more widespread roses and castles.

The only design remotely akin to a rose was a small eight-petalled star or flower which very often appeared on the coal boats, but in technique it owed more to the signwriter than the artist. The simplest version consisted of four strokes drawn into a central spot with a dash between each; the next stage was to replace the intermediate dash with a *fleur de lys*, or a full-sized petal stroke, and put an extra ring around the centre spot or round the perimeter; a very attractive pattern was the result. It was most commonly used on the top panels of the cabin doors, painted in white or cream in a red circle against a green background, but it appeared on the shoulders and fore end as well. It appeared through-out the Black Country as the only concession to floral decoration and was very effective.

Fig. 28 *Five variations of the eight petalled star or flower that appears throughout the BCN. Individual boat builders' work could be identified by their star or 'spider'.*

132

It is worth remembering that BCN day-boats were very similar in construction to the earliest canal narrow boat, as can be seen from contemporary specifications, and it is possible that they looked very similar. Accepting this, it is also possible that their paintwork was in direct descent from the decoration of the earliest boats. This idea would have added credence if the colliery boats around the Worsley area, Manchester, which are also survivors of an earlier simple boatbuilding style, evolved by James Brindley, showed similar tendencies. Alas, any decoration is notable in its complete absence.

APPENDIX I

In September 1858, the weekly magazine *Household Words* published a three part article, 'On the Canal' by John Hollingshead. It gives us perfect and clear proof that the tradition of roses and castles existed then and was already recognised as something out of the ordinary. Elsewhere, it shows that the cabin layout then was in all major features the same as it is today, and that family boating was an accepted system on the canals, even if not with the Grand Junction Company on whose boat Mr Hollingshead travelled.

> The *Stourport* is rather faded in its decorations, and is not a gay specimen of the fly-barge in all its glory of cabin paint and varnish; but still enough remains to show what it was in its younger days, and what it will be again when it gets a week in dock for repairs, at Birmingham. The boatman lavishes all his taste; all his rude, uncultivated love for the *fine* arts, upon the external and internal ornaments of his floating home. His chosen colours are red, yellow and blue; all so bright that, when newly laid on and appearing under the rays of a mid-day sun, they are too much for the unprotected eye of the unaccustomed stranger. The two sides of the cabin, seen from the bank, and the towing-path, present a couple of landscapes, in which there is a lake, a castle, a sailing-boat, and a range of mountains, painted after the style of the *great teaboard* school of art. If the *Stourport* cannot match many of its companions in the freshness of its cabin decorations, it can eclipse every other barge upon the canal in the brilliancy of a new two-gallon water-can, shipped from a bank-side painter's yard, at an early period of the journey. It displayed no fewer than six dazzling and fanciful composition landscapes, several gaudy wreaths of flowers, and the name of its proud proprietor, Thomas Randle, running round the centre upon a back-ground of blinding yellow.

APPENDIX 2

Part of Chapter 1 of 'Life on the Upper Thames' by H. R. Robertson, published in 1873 in the *Art Journal*. Although rather romantic, his description of the castles on the cabin side seem to be the result of first-hand observation, and suggests that they were pretty primitive, the work of an untutored painter rather than a professional artist.

> The exterior decoration of these boats is noticeable, and evinces the pride taken in their appearance by their owners, who repaint them with the gayest colours as often as they can afford to do so. On the outside of the cabin are painted two or four landscapes (usually river-scenes), of which they are proud enough; and it is curious they invariably speak of them as 'cuts'. The one in our illustration is faithfully copied, and shows a river in which the water makes no attempt to find its own level, one side of the stream appearing many feet higher than the other. The tree might stagger a botanist, but the whole serves its first purpose as a cheerful decoration, which our more pretentious art so frequently misses. The smartness of the cabin part of the barge is often the more striking from the fact that the load it bears is of a very opposite character, as coal, which is perhaps the most common freight.

APPENDIX 3

The following extract was printed in the *Birmingham Daily Mail* in March 1875, as part of an article publicising Mr George Smith's attempts to get the Canal Boats Acts passed. The 'gay pictorial pail' I assume to be a handbowl, and I think the writer must have seen an example of a cavalier/crusader painting to describe it; the accepted subject matter for the canal painter then seemed to be excitingly broad.

I have noted by this time the strange love of the boatman for pictorial display. He likes the outer shell of his cabin bedaubed in streaks of gay colour. Inside he rejoices in highly illuminated panels, he affects a gay pictorial pail the top rim of which is embellished by a painted garland of small flowers; the body is enriched by designs of outrageous roses and sunflowers; while the bottom offers a good ground whereupon to depict a gay cavalier or valiant crusader in full armour. Any and every article serves as a 'ground' for the lavish display of the canal boat artist.

APPENDIX 4

In a book *British Manufacturing Industries* of 1876 there is an article by a Mr Lindsay dealing with the papier-maché trade, including interesting comments on the development of decorative paintwork fashions of the 1830s and 40s, and their subsequent commercialism.

In 1832 another style of ornamentation was introduced by the firm of JENNENS and BETTERIDGE. Up to that period the flowers introduced upon papier-maché were not imitations of nature, but a sort of Chinese impasto ornament. Natural flowers were now painted upon the centre of the article to which was given a border of light ornamental gold work. This was regarded by the trade as a bold step, but it seemed to hit the public taste, and the patterns put into the market continued to sell freely for nearly thirty years.

A paragraph further on we have:

In 1845 a new and pleasing style of ornamentation of papier-maché articles was adopted at the Old Hall Work at Wolverhampton and had a marvellous run for a number of years. This was the selection of interior and exterior view of the old baronial halls of England, and the various cathedrals.

A few more sentences will sum up the gist of Mr Lindsay's article, and point to the steady deterioration of taste in this field, paralleled by other goods produced for the working class market.

> . . . a morbid taste arose in the Birmingham japan trade for placing great blotches of pearl upon articles made of pulp, and finishing them in the gaudiest of colours. Certain manufacturers finding it more profitable, for the moment, neglected the production of better and more carefully studied work; and pearl landscapes, pearl ruins, and pearl flowers and fruit seemed destined to supersede the admirable artistic productions of such men as Haseler, McCallum, Stanier and others.
>
> The old, showy, gaudy, unnatural style of flower decoration will now only sell, at most unremunerative prices, amongst the lower classes of society in Europe and among the uncivilised masses in other countries.

APPENDIX 5

This is an extract from Chapter 3 of L. T. C. Rolt's book *Narrow Boat* which did so much to reawaken interest in the canals after World War II. It was first published by Eyre & Spottiswoode in 1944, and this excerpt beautifully describes the decorative work being done at Tooley's dockyard in Banbury just before the war. It is so complete that I can offer no useful comment, except to thank Mr Rolt for allowing me to quote it in full.

When the heavier jobs on the hull have been completed, the boat-builder's next task is the re-decoration, and I was lucky enough to see this work carried out on the boat *Florence*, which was on the dock at the time of my arrival. Each member of the family played his special part. George began in his spare time from the factory; he was the lettering expert, and painted the owner's name and port of origin in elaborate cream lettering, shaded with blue, on the large vermilion centre panel of the cabin side. Then it was the old man's turn to embellish his son's work with little garlands of bright flowers in the four corners and between the lettering. Finally it was left to Herbert, the younger son, to paint his castles on the four small side panels. Apart from striking a line with a chalked string to keep the lettering level, they did no preliminary sketching or spacing out whatever, but worked straight out of their heads with wonderful rapidity and skill. I watched fascinated while Herbert painted the four castles in the space of one afternoon. Dipping first into one and then another of the small tins of oil paint of his own grinding and mixing, he blended together the green, the blue and the sepia until a typical scene, dear to generations of canal folk, suddenly took shape under his hand. Here it would be a castle with a single battlement turret, rising against a background of rolling blue hills and red sunset; there a more monastic structure, twin towered, and backed by woods, a stream flowing improbably through an arch in the base of one tower and spreading into a lake in the foreground. Each panel differed from its neighbour, yet all were true to that traditional form which appears so strangely foreign in its conception. Who first established this convention of tall stuccoed towers and wide-eaved red roofs? Perhaps it was some old wandering Romany who exchanged his caravan for a narrow boat when the canals were young, and adorned the walls of his new home with his memories of fairy-castles in the Carpathians. Whatever the origin, its influence is still strong, for this was by no means the end of the decorative work. Castles were also painted on the inside of the cabin doors and in the cabin itself, while the 'ram's head', the tiller bar and the 'stands' and 'cratches' which support the gangplanks all had to be picked out with bright geometrical patterns of colour before the boatman's exacting eye was satisfied.

Each boat carries two water-cans, one as open 'dipper' which, as its name implies, is dipped into the canal and used for a hundred and one domestic uses, from peeling potatoes to washing the captain's wool vest; the other is a tall can with handle, spout and lid, like a mammoth hot-water jug, in which drinking-water is stored. Both are elaborately decorated with flowers, and often carry the owner's name in white letters on a red circumferential band. The boatmen brought these cans to Mr Tooley when they needed a repaint, for the old man excelled at this work. To behold him, as I did, when he sat before the bench in his narrow workshop, the battered bowler firmly planted on the back of his head and a tray of many-coloured paints at his elbow, was to see the past miraculously living in the present. Not a past preserved in a museum or spuriously recreated in an Art and Craft shop, but a vital tradition. Handling his fine camel-hair brushes with wonderful sureness and delicacy, he first of all painted little shaded discs of sepia, ochre and pink on the green ground of the can and surrounded them with a garland of pale green leaves. These were the centres of the roses. When they were dry, the petals, red on sepia, yellow on ochre, and white on pink, were superimposed so simply and swiftly that only in the way a mere blob of paint seemed suddenly to blossom forth was the skill revealed. The bright work was completed when the veining of the leaves had been painted in with a very fine brush and a coat of varnish applied to preserve it.

ACKNOWLEDGEMENTS

I should like to acknowledge the debt that I owe to the many individuals and museums who have helped me with this book. I want to thank everyone in the following long list, all of whom have taken considerable trouble to help me with information, but my thanks are no less for having to be given to so many: Abington Museum, Northampton; Tommy Appleton; Charlie Atkins; Harry Bentley; Birmingham City Museum; Nigel Carter; Ted Chetwynd; Harry Crook; George Crowshaw; Peter Dorleijn; Dudley Library and Museum; Sheila Gordon; Charles Hadfield; C. N. Hadlow; Harry Hanson; Harold Hood; Ron Hough; Mr Howard of Taylor's dock, Chester; Barbara Jones; Yvonne Jones, Keeper of Bantock House Museum, Wolverhampton; Ken Keay, for much of the information in chapter 5; Mike LeRoy; Harry Leyland; Travers Lisney; City of Liverpool Museum, whose staff have been a constant source of help; Manchester Museum; Mr and Mrs A. H. Owen; Jess Owen; Philip Pacey; Mr and Mrs L. T. C. Rolt; Max Savage; Jacqueline Schoevers; Geoff Taylor; Jack Taylor; George Wain; Warrington Library, Jim Yates.

In particular I should like to thank Mary Prior for the many valuable references she gave me, the result of her own scholarly research, Robert Wilson who generously put all his own notes on the subject at my disposal as well as helping with the photographs, Harry Arnold who did a great deal of photographic work for me, and Richard Hutchings who allowed me full use of the British Waterways collection at Stoke Bruerne Museum. Finally I should like to thank Edward Paget-Tomlinson for helping and encouraging my research in very many ways throughout.

BIBLIOGRAPHY

De Voe, Shirley Spaulding. *English Papier Maché of the Georgian and Victorian Periods* (1971)

Fastnedge, Ralph. *Sheraton Furniture* (1962)

Faulkner, Alan. *The George and the Mary* (1973)

Jenkins, J. Geraint. *The English Farm-Wagon* (Reading 1961)

Hadfield, Charles. *British Canals* (1969)

Hansen, H. J. (editor) *European Folk Art* (1968)

Hornell, James. *Water Transport* (reprinted Newton Abbot 1970)

Johns, W. D. and Simcox, Anne. *Pontypool and Usk Japanned Wares* (Newport, Mon. 1953)

Jones, Barbara. *The Unsophisticated Arts* (1951)

Lethbridge, T. C. *Boats and Boatmen* (1952)

McKnight, Hugh. *Canal and River Craft in Pictures* (Newton Abbot 1969)

O'Connor, John. *Canals, Barges and People* (1950)

Robacker, Earl F. *Touch of the Dutchland* (1965)

Rolt, L. T. C. *Narrow Boat* (1944)

Sabine, Ellen S. *American Folk Art* (New York 1958)

Smith, George. *Our Canal Population* (1879)

Vale, Edmund. *By Shank and Crank* (1924)

Ward-Jackson, C. H. and Harvey, Denis E. *The English Gypsy Caravan* (Newton Abbot 1972)

Wilson, Robert. *The Number Ones* (Kettering 1972)

Magazines and Periodicals

Art Journal, 1873, H. R. Robertson, 'Life on the Upper Thames'

Burlington Magazine, Vol 49, 1926. Camilla Doyle, 'The Vanishing Arts of a Peasantry'

The Countryman, Summer 1949. Frederick Burgess, 'Roses, Castles and Lozenges'

Household Words, 18 September 1858. John Hollingshead, 'On the Canal'

Lock and Quay, house magazine of the Docks & Inland Waterways
Executive. Interesting references to narrow boat painting in
copies dated:
    December 1949 'Our Front Cover'
    April 1953 'Colour on the Canal'
    April 1954 'Round the Waterways, NW Div'
    July 1954 'Maintaining British Waterways Craft'
Man Royal Anthropological Institute, August 1955. C. F. Tebbutt
FSA 'Some Cart and Wagon Decorations of the British Isles and
Eire'

Unpublished Sources
Hanson, Harry. 'The Canal Boatmen 1760–1914', thesis presented
for M.A. degree at Manchester University 1973.
Pacey, Philip. 'Folk, Baroque and Pop', dissertation presented as
part of degree course at Cambridge University 1967.

INDEX

Page numbers in italic refer to illustrations

Printed in the USA
CPSIA information can be obtained
at www.ICGtesting.com
JSHW052018140824
68134JS00027B/2538